L'Anconitana

The Woman from Ancona

L'Anconitana

The Woman from Ancona

Ruzante
(Angelo Beolco)

TRANSLATED

WITH AN INTRODUCTION

AND NOTES BY

NANCY DERSOFI

UNIVERSITY
OF CALIFORNIA
PRESS

BERKELEY
LOS ANGELES
LONDON

University of California Press
Berkeley and Los Angeles, California

University of California Press, Ltd.
London, England
© 1994 by
The Regents of the University of California

The Italian text of *L'Anconitana* is reprinted from Ruzante, *Teatro,* edited by Ludovico Zorzi (Turin: Giulio Einaudi Editore, 1967), by permission of the publisher.

Library of Congress Cataloging-in-Publication Data

Ruzzante, 1496?–1542.
  [Anconitana. English & Italian]
  L'Anconitana = The woman from Ancona / Ruzzante (Angelo Beolco); translated with an introduction and notes by Nancy Dersofi.
     p.   cm.—(Biblioteca italiana)
  Italian text and English translation on facing pages.
  Includes bibliographical references.
  ISBN 0-520-08525-6 (alk. paper).—
  ISBN 0-520-08526-4 (pbk.: alk. paper)
  I. Dersofi, Nancy. II. Title. III. Title: Woman from Ancona. IV. Series.
PQ4610.B47A62   1994
852'.3—dc20   93-35922
                                               CIP

Printed in the United States of America
9 8 7 6 5 4 3 2 1

The paper used in this publication meets the minimum requirements of American National Standard for Information Sciences—Permanence of Paper for Printed Library Materials, ANSI Z39.48-1984.

TO MYRNA, PHYLLIS, AND JUDY

Contents

Acknowledgments

THIS TRANSLATION AND THE FRAME I set it in have
evolved over so long a time that it is impossible to thank
by name everyone who has lent a hand. Dante Della
Terza first recommended that I translate Ruzante when
he and Harry Levin directed my Harvard dissertation on
the actor-playwright. While making that dissertation
into a book, I consulted in Italy with Mario Baratto,
Ludovico Zorzi, and Emilio Menegazzo. At Bryn Mawr,
Charles Mitchell encouraged my further work on Ruzante. Louise George Clubb has contributed generously
to this project. Giorgio Padoan and Richard Hamilton
reviewed the Introduction. James Haar has answered
many questions about Renaissance music. Marisa Milani
has kindly shared her linguistic research.

A fellowship in 1976–77 at Villa I Tatti enabled me
to study Ruzante's songs. The Gladys Krieble Delmas
Foundation supported a stay in Padua, where I photo-
graphed and studied the Loggia and Odeon Cornaro.

In assembling an international community of special-
ists for three conferences on Ruzante in 1983, 1987, and
1990, Giovanni Calendoli has aided Ruzante studies im-
measurably; I am grateful to him and the *comune* of
Padua for inviting my participation. For persuading me,
by directing and performing wonderfully in an early version of this translation, that *The Woman from Ancona* had
a future, I thank Andrew Lichtenberg, first director of
theater at Bryn Mawr and Haverford colleges. The er-
rors are my own.

Note on the Text

THERE ARE TWO MANUSCRIPT COPIES of *L'Anconitana*, one in the Marciana Library in Venice, the other in the Civic Library of Verona. The manuscripts are virtually identical except that in the Venetian manuscript the eulogy to Padua is offered instead to Venice. This discrepancy may be a gesture of *campanilismo* on the part of the Venetian copyist or a change made for a performance in Venice. The text I have followed is in Ruzante, *Teatro*, ed. Ludovico Zorzi (Turin: Einaudi, 1967), pp. 773–881. Zorzi discusses the manuscripts and early printed editions in his "Nota al testo," p. 1621. While the manuscripts divide the text into five acts, Zorzi divided each act into scenes and added stage directions. I have included the scene divisions and stage directions in my translation. Although I have tried to stay close to the Italian, to the Venetian, and to Ruzante's "bon pavan," I have varied the translation of some repeated words (*virtù* and *cancaro* in particular) in response to their sense and for a more natural English version. I have used the dialect spelling of the name "Ruzante" rather than the Italian "Ruzzante."

Introduction

FAMOUS DURING HIS LIFETIME for his stage portrayal of
a rustic from the countryside north of Padua, Angelo
Beolco, called Ruzante, wrote a series of plays using
his character's native dialect, Pavano. Author and actor,
Ruzante took his name from the character he played
in monologues, dialogues, and short rustic comedies
dramatizing the hard realities and natural pleasures of
country life. His longer plays experiment with pastoral
drama and the new genre of vernacular comedy modeled on Plautus and Terence. Speaking their native Pavano, Ruzante and his companion rustics mingle with
characters who speak Venetian, Bergamask, or, as in
L'Anconitana, the newly established standard Italian.
Ruzante's plurilingual theater gave the Italian stage a
model for the dialect characters and virtuoso acting that
were carried on in *commedia dell'arte.* Complex textures,
intersecting plots, and high tones played against low give
his theater dimensions that came to characterize European theater in its fullest flower; similar themes and
characters in *L'Anconitana* and Shakespeare's *As You
Like It,* for example, illustrate the technique intrinsic to
European Renaissance comedy of putting new wine in
old casks—that is, of borrowing theatrical elements or
"theatergrams," from play to play.

Ruzante's theater also encompasses the Renaissance
idea of theater as an architectural space. While performing at private palaces in Venice and Padua as well as at
the ducal courts of Ferrara (where he collaborated with
Ariosto), Ruzante wrote for a theater that commands its
own place, whether an open-air theater on the ancient
model or the mythical realm of Legraçion (Mirth) imag-
ined in his final work. An interest in ancient theatrical

1

architecture led his patron, Alvise Cornaro, to build a theater in imitation of antiquity in the courtyard of his Paduan home. Ruzante helped to renew the ancient belief, codified by Vitruvius, that the theater has a fixed place in the social life of the community and in its architecture.

Ruzante performed his first play, the verse *Pastoral,* in Padua around 1518, when the Studio (as the University of Padua was called) reopened at the end of the wars of Cambrai.[1] In *La Pastoral,* Ruzante, a *contadino* (tenant farmer) from the Pavano, confronts Italian-speaking shepherds and a farcical Bergamask doctor. Having asserted a lead over the shepherds and clowns in the *Pastoral,* Ruzante remains the central character in works that take country love and marriage or the horror of war and famine for themes; the longer plays adapt rustic figures to the conventions of Roman comedy. In all but the final work—the *Littera de Ruzante a Messier Marco Alvarotto,* recounting Ruzante's journey to the kingdom of Legraçion (Mirth)—Ruzante speaks Pavano; in the *Letter* he is guided in a dream by a former Pavano-speaking comedian called Barba Polo, but Ruzante narrates the event in Italian. After signing the *Letter* on the day of Epiphany 1536 with his theatrical name, "Ruzante," Angelo Beolco wrote nothing more until he died, still young, in 1542 while preparing to act in Sperone Speroni's academic tragedy *La Canace.*

From the outset, Ruzante's singular appreciation of rustic characters speaking their native tongue characterized his theater and its reputation. At the end of

1. Giorgio Padoan, "Angelo Beolco da Ruzante a Perduoçimo," in *Momenti del Rinascimento veneto* (Padua: Antenore, 1978), pp. 95–105. This article was first published in *Lettere italiane* 20 (1968): 121–200. It discusses the evidence and issues involved in dating Ruzante's complete works.

the sixteenth century Galileo Galilei, who had lived in Padua for eighteen years, enjoyed reading Ruzante's dialect aloud to friends.[2] In the eighteenth century, the comedian *dell'arte* Luigi Riccoboni wrote that Ruzante's reputation withstood his having introduced to comedy "the most barbarous languages in Italy."[3] When Maurice and George Sand revived Ruzante's work in the nineteenth century at their theater in Nohant, they translated the plays into French; in Italy, Ruzante's dialect was translated into Italian. Modern interest has focused again on the dialects and on the use of popular forms, alone or superimposed on erudite forms, which uniquely explore the realities of contemporary life in the countryside, where war, plunder, and famine had turned life upside down or, in Ruzante's idiom, "ass end up."

Ruzante boasts that his "bon pavan" is worth more than "two hundred Florentines," a pun on a coin in circulation in the sixteenth century and on the cultural movement to make Tuscan the literary standard. In prologues and monologues Ruzante tells his aristocratic and scholarly audiences that he would rather speak naturally, in Pavano, than behave like those "vegeta-balls, who try to look literary and erudite by calling sheep farmers shepherds and speaking Florentine until—blood of the Antichrist!—they make me laugh in my pants."[4]

2. See Emilio Lovarini, "Galileo interprete del Ruzzante," in *Studi sul Ruzzante e sulla letteratura pavana,* ed. G. Folena (Padua: Antenore, 1965), pp. 377–392.

3. Luigi Riccoboni, *Discorso della commedia all'improvviso e scenari inediti,* ed. I. Mamczarz (Milan: Il Polifilo, 1973), p. 28.

4. Ruzante, *Teatro,* ed. Ludovico Zorzi (Turin: Einaudi, 1967), p. 153: "Né gnian guardè che a' vuogia far com fa non so che cogómbari, che vuò mostrare de essere sletràn sinçiè, che i vuò dire de pegorari, che igi i ciama pastore, e sí favela da Fiorenza, che i me fa, al sangue di l'Anticristo! cagar da riso da per tuto."

In particular, he champions his country dialect against the bookish, unnatural language sponsored by Pietro Bembo, whose influential *Prose della volgar lingua* advocates a vernacular based on the writings of Petrarch and Boccaccio. By imitating the harmonious sounds and rhythms of these great trecento authors, says Bembo, new writers may also compose perfectly and for eternity. Bembo's position, in the words of Dante Della Terza, "favors a concept of perennial contemporariness which stops time and, by excluding the impact of the present, hopes to exorcise the troublesome future."[5] Pietro Bembo may have been a spectator when Ruzante argued in favor of an alternative spoken vernacular.

Ruzante's stage language is in fact a stylized version of the dialect spoken in the countryside,[6] adapted for the stage and resonant with Rabelaisian obscenity. For example, a favorite expletive, *potta* (female genitalia), becomes a ritualized motif within a dialect as spoken in real life yet distorted in the spirit of carnival for comic effect. Plurilingualism further carnivalizes the plays' use of language. Ruzante's translator faces the problem of rendering the dialect in a tone that violates neither its theatricality nor its immediacy. A translator in England was admonished to "buy a mouthwash, a clean typewriter and a dictionary" for having limited himself to four-letter versions of Ruzante's inventive expletives.[7] Ru-

5. Dante Della Terza, introduction to *Arcadia and the Stage: An Introduction to the Dramatic Art of Angelo Beolco, Called Ruzante,* by N. Dersofi (Madrid: Porrua; Washington, D.C.: Studia Humanitatis, 1978), p. 3.

6. See Marisa Milani, "Snaturalitè e deformazione nella lingua teatrale del Ruzante," in *Lingue e strutture del teatro italiano del Rinascimento* (Padua: Liviana, 1970), pp. 109–202.

7. Review of Angelo Beolco (Il Ruzante), *The Comedy without a Title,* translated and adapted by Harold Hobson, at the Lyric Theatre, Hammersmith, in the *Times Literary Supple-*

zante's language does not merely shock; indeed, many of his linguistic effects derive from one voice parodying another, establishing unlikely relationships or, as Mario Baratto observed of the *Pastoral,* revealing the inability of the authentic rustic to communicate with the literary shepherd.[8] In *L'Anconitana* Ruzante plays opposite a Venetian merchant and young lovers who speak a literary sort of Italian; he celebrates his own Pavano in a prologue and in songs woven into the text.

By championing a spoken dialect against literary Tuscan, the playwright stood in radical opposition to linguistic standardization and centralization. Yet the language question per se was remote from real concerns of peasant life in the sixteenth century, whereas Ruzante's characterization, like his language, is rooted in country life and belongs to the history of the Pavano. From the time Venice annexed Padua in 1405, the surrounding countryside had felt the landward development of the Venetian empire. Venetians began purchasing land on the Terraferma toward the end of the fifteenth century when Venice's mercantile position in the Mediterranean began to diminish. Agriculture and mainland industries then became increasingly important until, by the middle of the seventeenth century, Venice found its main economic support on the mainland.[9] The takeover of farmland from smallholders was facilitated by hardships brought on by the wars of the League of Cambrai,

ment, June 3, 1983, p. 571. I thank Joan Hartman for calling this review to my attention.

8. Mario Baratto, "Ruzante," in *Tre saggi sul teatro* (Venice: Neri Pozza, 1964), p. 55; first published as "L'esordio di Ruzante," *Revue des études italiennes,* n.s., 3 (1956): 92–162, nn. 2–3.

9. See Oliver Logan, *Culture and Society in Venice, 1470–1790* (New York: Scribner's, 1972), p. 21.

which was formed to strip Venice of her mainland territory. In May 1509, the league won a decisive victory at Agnadello, forcing Venice to surrender Padua to the Emperor Maximilian I, a move supported by landowners descended from Padua's feudal nobility; but the following July a band of Venetians recaptured the city. Farmers, dependent on Venetian markets, sided with Venice against the imperial forces, and by all accounts fought bravely for the republic; nevertheless, plunder, famine, and disease drove them from their land. Although some *contadini* occupied abandoned monasteries and returned to the countryside when fighting abated, renewed fighting and the arrival of fresh mercenaries in 1510 continued to force farmers off their land.[10] Country men and women fled to Padua or Venice, where they became the servants of new masters.

Interpreters of Ruzante's plays have puzzled over the author's attitude toward the historical figure on whom his character is based: does Ruzante satirize the "gutter-aloid Calibans of the Paduan countryside,"[11] or does he champion their cause? Actor and thus interpreter of Ruzante's roles, the author continually revised his character, from play to play, and possibly from one performance to another, altering his character over time as he responded to the farmers' changing world and to his

10. The flight of peasant refugees into Venice is discussed in Felix Gilbert, *The Pope, His Banker, and Venice* (Cambridge: Harvard University Press, 1980), pp. 17–18.

11. Translated from Gianfranco Contini, *saggio introduttivo* to *La cognizione del dolore,* by Carlo Emilio Gadda (Turin: Einaudi, 1963), pp. 20, 22; cited in Mario Baratto, "Da Ruzante al Beolco: Per la storia di un autore," in *Atti del convegno sul tema: La poesia rusticana nel Rinascimento,* Problemi attuali di scenza e di cultura (Rome: Accademia Nazionale dei Lincei, 1969), p. 92.

own;[12] indeed, separating author from actor and actor
from character has been a central concern of modern
criticism, which has searched Beolco's life for clues. But
biographical information is scarce. Angelo Beolco was
born in Padua around 1496,[13] the illegitimate son of
Giovanni Francesco Beolco, a member of Padua's upper
class. Angelo's paternal grandfather, a merchant of Mil-
anese descent, was successful enough in the cloth trade
and the new printing industry to attain Paduan citizen-
ship and educate his sons at the Studio. His older son,
Giovanni Francesco Beolco, was awarded a doctorate in
arts in 1485, a year after his father's death; in 1513 he
completed a second degree, in medicine. An associate of
the college of medicine and arts from 1493, he served as
a prior of the university in 1500 and again in 1513–14.
Angelo Beolco was probably born in the period after
his grandfather's death when his father, not yet married,

12. The author's changing attitude toward his character is
discussed in Giovanni Calendoli, *Ruzante* (Venice: Corbo e
Fiore, 1985), pp. 33–52.

13. An inscription by Giovanni Battista Rota for Beolco's
tomb in the Church of San Daniele in Padua, known only in
a version published by Bernardino Scardeone in *De antiquitate urbis Patavii et claris civibus Patavinis* (Basel, 1560), p. 255
(quoted in Emilio Lovarini, "Le canzoni popolari in Ruzante
e in altri scrittori alla pavana del secolo XVI," in *Studi sul Ruzzante,* ed. G. Folena, p. 167), says that Beolco died on March
17, 1542, at the age of forty. However, because Beolco signed
a legal document in 1521 that required him to be twenty-five
years old, it is generally assumed that he was born not later
than 1496. Archival research on Beolco and proposals for a
biography are published in E. Menegazzo and P. Sambin,
"Nuove esplorazioni archivistiche per Angelo Beolco e Alvise
Cornaro," *Italia medioevale e umanistica* 7 (1964): 133–247;
and 9 (1966): 229–385. See also E. Menegazzo, "Tre scritti di
Alvise Cornaro," in *Tra Latino e Volgare* per Carlo Dionisotti,
Medioevo e umanesimo 17–18 (1974): 585–613.

still resided in his paternal home. Angelo's mother may have been a young maidservant employed by his grandmother, the widow Paola Beolco, who protected Angelo's interests after his father married and fathered six legitimate children (one of whom died in infancy). Legal documents indicate that Angelo's father gave him his power of attorney in 1521. When he died (before 1525) Giovanni Francesco left his firstborn son a modest inheritance of twenty-five ducats, a glass generally perceived as half empty. In 1526 Giovanni Francesco's widow and children settled a larger sum on Angelo and appointed him their estate manager. Angelo also managed country estates for Alvise Cornaro, a wealthy landowner in the region and a figure central to Paduan cultural life and to Beolco's career.

Claiming that his Venetian descent was from a noble line, Alvise Cornaro petitioned Venice more than once, without success, for the privileges of nobility. In Padua he imitated the life-style of Venice's nobility, his patronage of Beolco and of the architect Giovan Maria Falconetto examples of the patrician style he favored. Archival information hints uncertainly at the nature of Cornaro's relationship to Ruzante: when Beolco was unable to pay for two expensive horses he purchased in 1526 and 1527, Cornaro paid the debt; it is not known, however, whether Beolco bought the horses to indulge an extravagance beyond his means or to meet a practical need for swift travel in the countryside. By 1527 Angelo had married a woman of modest circumstances named Giustina Palatino, although she continued to live in her parents' home. From 1521 until his death, Ruzante resided in Cornaro's Paduan home and country estates, where he shared the companionship of artists and literati, among them Pietro Bembo, who said in a letter to Cornaro dated July 4, 1528, that he envied his friend his

pleasant life with "il vostro buono e dolcissimo Messer Angelo" (your good and most gentle Master Angelo).[14] Ruzante died in 1542, possibly from malaria contracted while supervising land-reclamation projects for Cornaro in the salt marshes and swamplands between Padua and Venice.

Surely the social and cultural programs sponsored by Cornaro, a Venetian, avoided rekindling anti-Venetian feeling among Padua's aristocracy, a group that was hostile to Venice in the Cambraic wars and punished in its aftermath. In Ruzante's family two of his half-brothers were condemned by Venice—one exiled to Ferrara, the other held in the prison adjoining the ducal palace. Guest performances that Ruzante gave in Venice early in his career with various *compagnie della calza* (companies of the hose: fraternities of young noblemen who entertained at civic and private festivities, taking their general name from their practice of wearing the same color or decoration on one trouser leg) ended abruptly in 1527, presumably because the comedian expressed anti-Venetian sentiment or engaged in activities against the republic. In Padua, he and his companion Paduan gentlemen, "nobiles iuvenes Patavini,"[15] established a kind of mainland fraternity on the Venetian model. Support of their enterprise would have served Cornaro's humanist interests and noble aspirations. It is an enigma, though, that while living amid the fellowship provided by Alvise Cornaro's congenial world, dependent on the labor of others, Angelo Beolco gave voice to the laborer. When the comedian recited a monologue at Barco d'Asolo to celebrate Francesco Cornaro's eleva-

14. An excerpt from the letter is published in Alfred Mortier, *Ruzzante* (Paris: J. Peyronnet, 1925), vol. 1, p. 35, n. 2.

15. Scardeone, *De antiquitate urbis Patavii,* p. 255.

tion to the office of cardinal in 1528, he reminded the cardinal of the command upon Adam to eat his bread by the sweat of his brow: "Today," says Ruzante, "we sweat and have nothing while those doing nothing are the ones who eat."[16]

Ruzante's powerful *Parlamento* dramatizes the burden that war had added to the natural hardships of country life. "What do you think it's like over there," he asks his companion, "where you don't know anyone, you don't know where to go, where people are saying: 'Kill, kill! Let him have it! Let him have it!'? Artillery, explosions, crossbows, arrows; you see one comrade killed, another dead at your feet."[17] Returning from battle, Ruzante goes to Venice to find the wife he had left behind, but in Venice he discovers that she no longer needs or wants him. The wars of Cambrai had in fact changed the lives of farmers who lost their lands and were forced to seek a livelihood in the cities. Their women, like Ruzante's wife, Gnua, also needed "a' magne ogni dí" (to eat every day).

L'Anconitana finds Ruzante after the wars in the service of an aged Venetian broker sojourning in Padua for the fresh air. Because the play portrays Ruzante as servant to this Venetian master, the twentieth-century stage revival of Ruzante's theater has made *L'Anconitana* a test case for the playwright's partisan sympathies. Modern performances of the play began in 1927, when Jacques Copeau's French version toured with great success in

16. Ruzante, *Teatro,* p. 1217: "Mo el me pare mo cha la vaghe a un altro muò, cha nu, che a' se suóm, a' no n'aón me, e gi altri, cha no se sua, el magne."

17. Ruzante, *Teatro,* p. 527: "Che criu che sipia a esser in quel paese? Che te no cognussi negun, te no sè don' andare, e che te vi' tanta zente che dise: 'Amaza, amaza! Dàghe, dàghe!' Trelarí, s-ciopiti, balestre, freçe; e te vi' qualche to compagno morto amazò, e quel'altro amazarete a pè."

France, Belgium, and Switzerland. The famous French actor portrayed Ruzante as a forerunner of the wily, self-interested *commedia dell'arte* servant, emphasizing his character's association with improvised comedy by adding an opening pantomime and a closing divertissement. Two years later Charles Dullin staged *Bilora,* a short play in whose closing scene the rustic character, Bilora, stabs his wife's Venetian seducer/employer to death. Critics said that *Bilora*'s realism anticipated Verga's *verismo.*[18]

In Italy, the stage revival of Ruzante's theater began early in the twentieth century with Ruzante's dialect translated into Italian. In the 1940s and 1950s, the actor Cesco Baseggio gave brilliant performances, adapting Ruzante's dialect to his own native Venetian. Thereafter, Italian directors determined that the plays should be performed by actors trained in the pronunciation, cadence, and gestures of Ruzante's Pavano. To carry out this plan and correct the lingering misimpression of Ruzante as a *commedia dell'arte* servant, Gianfranco DeBosio and Ludovico Zorzi toured in France and Belgium in 1965–66 with a production of *L'Anconitana* on a double bill with *Bilora.*[19] Their program enabled the directors to present a resilient, urbanized Ruzante alongside a rustic Bilora—powerless, humiliated, and cowardly in his violence.

Beolco's original method of combining linguistic and stylistic voices echoes in this and in more recent ap-

18. See Giovanni Calendoli, "Antefatti di una fortuna difficile," in *Ruzante sulle scene italiane del secondo dopoguerra* (catalog for the exhibition at the Oratorio di San Rocco in Padua, May 25–June 15, 1983, sponsored by the Comune di Padova, Assessorato allo Spettacolo, and the Università degli Studi di Padova, Istituto di Storia del Teatro e dello Spettacolo), pp. 15–16.

19. See Gianfranco DeBosio, "Un trentennio di lavoro sul Ruzante," in *Ruzante sulle scene italiane,* pp. 36–39.

11

proaches taken by stage directors, who seem to find that no single work expresses Ruzante's image of the rustic world. A 1985 production of *Bilora* directed by Angelo Savelli toured Italy and France with a dramatic cantata called "Canto della terra sospesa" (Song of Nowhere) based on a new text composed of scenes adapted from several plays. Musical instruments and singing voices accompanied the action, which was performed first in Pavano, then in Provençal.[20] With the text functioning as a kind of libretto reinforced by action, gestures, and music, the audience follows a tale that shows Ruzante falling in love, called to war, betrayed by his wife and friend, and driven finally to a desperate suicidal attempt to eat himself alive. The closing image of the character addressing the boots he has removed so he can devour himself feet first (and die well fed) is a stock moment in the actor's repertory.

Such virtuoso solo scenes focus on the actor, whose gestures, songs, and stock routines anticipate the techniques of improvised theater. Comedians *dell'arte* improvised dialogue from a scenario outlining a sequence of actions that form a plot. In performance, each character or *maschera* (mask) spoke his own dialect, generating the dialogic relationships in which Mikhail Bakhtin saw the origin of modern novelistic discourse. Ruzante wrote his plays in full—improvising, perhaps, in performance or rehearsal in a manner carried on in European theater by the English actor William Kemp, whose skills and talent shaped the role he played. As a director Ru-

20. This work was performed in Florence at the Cloister of Brunelleschi on July 4–7, 1985, during the thirty-eighth *Estate Fiesolana*. The production offered two versions of the same text: the first in the author's original Pavano; the second in the "lingua d'oc" as adapted for the *Théâtre de la Carriera* in Villeneuve-lès-Avignon.

zante rehearsed scrupulously, judging from his letter of January 23, 1532, to Duke Ercole d'Este of Ferrara assuring the duke that he would be glad to have Ariosto prepare the stage so he could travel with his actors by boat and have a final run-through. While this note offers a glimpse at a practical working relationship between Ruzante and the older Ludovico Ariosto, Ariosto's legacy is most deeply felt in the texts of Ruzante's plays.

When Ariosto offered the court at Ferrara a "new" comedy in 1508, original in plot and written in "volgar lingua" (the vernacular), he invited playwrights to imitate antiquity with plays responding to contemporary society in its local settings. A year later, in his prologue to *Suppositi,* Ariosto called his method "poetical imitation, not theft," although what began as a method for transposing the lessons of Plautus and Terence into the vernacular quickly led to a wholesale lifting of characters, scenes, lines, segments of plot, and everything else. Ariosto's *Suppositi* has echoes in one of its funniest successors, Bibbiena's *La Calandria* (1513), and both plays resonate in *L'Anconitana*.[21] Collaboration with Ariosto during Beolco's engagements at Ferrara in 1529 and 1532 may have encouraged the younger playwright to attempt the new genre on his own. His mastery of it is evident in his treatment of *L'Anconitana*'s title character, Ginevra, the woman from Ancona, in whom Ruzante reinvents one of the most pervasive figures to inhabit the Renaissance stage—a woman in male disguise.

The plot, reuniting the long-lost sisters Isotta and Ginevra, recalls Plautus's much-copied *Menaechmi,* where male twins are mistaken for one another and finally re-

21. See Giorgio Padoan, "L'*Anconitana* tra Boccaccio, Bibbiena e Ariosto," in *Momenti del Rinascimento veneto* (Padua: Antenore, 1978), pp. 274–283; first published in *Lettere italiane* 22 (1970): 100–105.

united. In *La Calandria,* Bibbiena made his interchange-
able twins male and female; thus when Ginevra's im-
mediate forerunner, Fulvia, cross-dresses to pursue her
lover Lidio, she is disappointed when instead of Lidio
she meets his female twin, Lidia, dressed like a man. In
the anonymous *Gl'Ingannati* of 1531 Lelia dresses like
a man to serve Flaminio, who spurns her, anticipating
Viola in *Twelfth Night,* who hides her love for the Duke
of Illyria beneath the mask of "Cesario." In male disguise these female characters learn new roles: either they
take fortune into their own hands or they attain an emi-
nence—one thinks of Rosalind in *As You Like It*—that
looks ahead to the transcendently virtuous character
in late Renaissance tragicomedy whom Louise George
Clubb has identified as the figure of woman as wonder.[22]

In *L'Anconitana* the action is divided between Ginevra, the woman from Ancona, and Ruzante, who speaks
of his passage from farm to war and finally to the city.
The play finds Ruzante and his Venetian master in Padua, where the aged Venetian seeks a tryst with a courtesan named Doralice. When Doralice's maidservant,
Bessa, turns out to be the lost love of Ruzante's country
youth, Ruzante arranges for the four of them to meet in
the nearby town of Arquà (ironically, where Petrarch
spent his final years). Intersecting the story of these dialect characters is a plot involving four young aristocrats
who love by the book, taking their inspiration from Petrarch and their language, names, and personal histories
from Boccaccio. Boccaccio's influence is immediately
apparent to an audience who recognizes that Ginevra
and Isotta take their names from "Ginevra la bella"

22. See Louise George Clubb, "Woman as Wonder," in
*Studies in the Continental Background of Renaissance English Lit-
erature,* ed. Dale B. J. Randall and George Walton Williams
(Durham, N.C.: Duke University Press, 1977), pp. 109–132.

and "Isotta la bionda" (fair Guinevere and blond Iseult) in *Decameron* X.vi, who achieved happy marriages after overcoming adversity. In *L'Anconitana* these women have been separated from childhood: Ginevra, married and widowed in Ancona, has fallen in love with Gismondo and followed him to Padua, not knowing that her adored Gismondo is really her own sister, Isotta, who had been captured by pirates and had adopted male disguise.[23] The name Gismondo does not appear in the *Decameron,* and the informed playgoer will realize that the name is a mask, although it is disconcerting that Gismondo/Isotta has fallen in love with a co-captive named Tancredi, whose name brings to mind the protagonist in *Decameron* IV.i, who forces the death of his daughter Ghismonda. Ruzante's plot, to be sure, uncovers Isotta's and Ginevra's sisterhood and concludes in happy marriages for Gismondo/Isotta with Tancredi and for Ginevra with Teodoro, borrowed from *Decameron* V.vii. The name Gismondo may further allude to a speaker in *Gl'Asolani,* Bembo's treatise on love presented in three dialogues set in the town of Asolo, where Caterina Cornaro, former queen of Cyprus, held court; thus the name alerts the audience that the play pays homage to Bembo's theories on love and language.

Ruzante's role in *L'Anconitana* displays his musicality, for the comedian was also a singer and composer of songs.[24] In 1529 Ruzante performed in Ferrara with a

23. This sibling relationship is discussed in N. Dersofi, "Comic Reflections," in *Renaissance Studies in Honor of Craig Hugh Smyth,* ed. Andrew Morrogh (Florence: Giunti Barbera, 1985), vol. 1, pp. 293–299.

24. The songs are published in Ruzante, *Teatro,* pp. 1255–1265; see also Lovarini, "Le canzoni popolari," especially pp. 165–236; Ludovico Zorzi, "Canzoni inedite del Ruzante," *Atti del Istituto Veneto di Scienze, Lettere ed Arti* 119

troupe of five other men and two women, who sang "*canzoni e madrigali*" in Pavano.[25] Nine of Ruzante's lyrics are extant, three of them set to music after his death by Adriano Willaert and one set by Filippo Azzaiolo. Because there is no information about the tunes Ruzante sang when he performed or how he accompanied them instrumentally, it is assumed that he sang his lyrics to music not written down, improvising tunes or borrowing them from Italian popular songs. Emilio Lovarini supposed that Ruzante used songs he learned from the *contadini,* citing Bernardino Scardeone's description of the playwright's gathering of "*rhythmos*" (that is, popular songs) during his travels in the countryside.[26] Nino Pirrotta notes that "most of the time Ruzante must have invented if not the tunes at least the words of his songs."[27]

Ruzante's singing voice, "el bel soran," was a top-part voice in the range associated today with the countertenor. A second line, called a *tenor,* added to the top voice (*cantus*) formed a *cantus-tenor* relationship that was, according to Pirrotta, a fundamental feature of music in the unwritten tradition known today as *frottola* music. This type of music adapted itself readily to a four-part

(1960–1961): 25–73; idem, "Note all'*Anconitana,*" Ruzante, *Teatro,* pp. 1468–1469, nn. 22–25; N. Dersofi, "Le canzoni del Ruzante e l'*Anconitana,*" in *Convegno internazionale di studi sul Ruzante,* ed. G. Calendoli and G. Velluci (Venice: Corbo e Fiore, 1987), pp. 49–54; idem, "Angelo Beolco," in *The New Grove Dictionary of Music and Musicians,* ed. Stanley Sadie (London: Macmillan, 1980).

25. Christofaro di Messibugo, *Banchetti, composizioni di vivande e apparecchio generale* (Ferrara, 1549); facsimile, ed. F. Bandini, Venice: Pozza, 1960), p. 50.

26. Scardeone, *De antiquitate urbis Patavii,* p. 255.

27. Nino Pirrotta and Elena Povoledo, *Music and Theatre from Poliziano to Monteverdi* (New York: Cambridge University Press, 1975), p. 84, n. 26.

texture, with the two lower voices either sung or played on an accompanying musical instrument, often the lute.[28] Thus Ruzante with one other singer (which his troupe always included) could sing in four-part harmony, or as Ruzante says when he asks his companion Menato to join him in a song: "*Nu du canto[n]la in quatro*" (the two of us will sing for four). Songs that could be performed by four voices or parts appear throughout Ruzante's plays. I suggest also that the notion of four voices singing as one has thematic importance in *L'Anconitana* and is a fundamental feature of Ruzante's theater.

Some fifty-two songs sung or mentioned in the plays ornament or epitomize the action. *L'Anconitana* is one of the most musical, with fourteen songs performed or cited. Only the rustic marriage play called *La Betía,* with fifteen songs, has a greater number. Moreover, the play's dramatic structure resembles four-part harmony, its characters, voices, and attitudes toward love ranging from high to low figuratively and linguistically, as if transposing four-part harmony into dramatic form. The two pairs of Tuscan-speaking lovers supply the top voices; Ruzante and Bessa, speaking Pavano, sound a middle tone; while Ruzante's master, Sier Tomao, speaks to the courtesan Doralice in a Venetian low voice. Each pair of lovers enacts a pattern of love distinct in language, goal, and tone. Although their differences fall

28. Ruzante's performance practices are discussed in Pirrotta and Povoledo, *Music and Theatre,* pp. 84 (and n. 26), 94, 99, and 100; see also H. Colin Slim, "Two Paintings of 'Concert Scenes' from the Veneto and the Morgan Library's Unique Music Print of 1520," in *In Cantu et in Sermone: For Nino Pirrotta on His 80th Birthday,* ed. F. Della Seta and F. Piperno (Florence: Olschki, 1989), pp. 155–174; and Howard M. Brown, "The Genesis of a Style: The Parisian Chanson, 1500–1530," in *Chanson and Madrigal: 1480–1530,* ed. James Haar (Cambridge: Harvard University Press, 1964), pp. 8–9.

into hierarchical order, they harmonize so that each voice brings out the quality of the others; together they sound as one.

This plan may illuminate the vexing question of *L'Anconitana*'s date of composition.[29] In the absence of external evidence, the play has been considered an early work like the multilingual *La Pastoral;* a middle-period work like the two plays modeled on Plautus, *La Piovana* (like *Rudens*) and *La Vaccaria* (like *Asinaria*); or a late work expressing the playwright's artistic maturity after an experimental period in which he produced his realistic masterpieces including *Bilora* and the powerful *Parlamento.* Here disagreement may be instructive. Is the play of two minds, the author's voice playing against the actor's? In *La Vaccaria* (1533) a character named Vezzo comments on the difference between architect and mason, reflecting an interest the playwright may have shared with Cornaro in architectural design and construction. An analogy to the different roles of author and actor is implied.

Musical harmony is related to the architectural plan and function of the theater where *L'Anconitana* was performed; indeed, the play may have inaugurated the final version of the Loggia and Odeon designed for Al-

29. The question of dating is addressed in Padoan, "Angelo Beolco," pp. 94–191; regarding L'*Anconitana* see especially pp. 171–191. Mario Baratto discusses the sequence of the works in "Da Ruzante al Beolco: Per la storia di un autore," in *Atti del convegno sul tema: La poesia rusticana nel Rinascimento,* Problemi attuali di scienza e di cultura (Rome: Accademia Nazionale dei Lincei, 1969), pp. 83–109. Articles linking L'*Anconitana* and *Betía* linguistically and conceptually by Marisa Milani ("Rileggendo Ruzzante: Note, ipotesi e provocazioni," in *Filologia veneta,* vol. 1, *Ruzzante* [Padova: Editoriale Programma, 1988], pp. 18–50) and musically by H. Colin Slim ("Two Paintings of 'Concert Scenes'") date L'*Anconitana* in the first quarter of the century.

vise Cornaro by the architect Giovan Maria Falconetto. These buildings follow Vitruvian principles of theatrical architecture and acoustics. The Loggia, built in 1524, was intended to imitate the *scaenae frons* of antiquity (fig. 1). About ten years later Cornaro added diagonally across from the Loggia an Odeon where music could be sung and played (fig. 2).[30] The buildings stand today in the courtyard of the house at Via Cesarotto 21, near the Santo, as the Basilica of Saint Anthony is called. Inside the rectangular Odeon there is an octagonal front room: four sides are open to natural light; the other four sides contain niches with benches. Sebastiano Serlio wrote that Cornaro and his family and friends had the Odeon built for music; of the octagonal room he says, "Here they play music, and the room is very suitable as it has a shape tending to roundness and is all vaulted with

30. The date of the Loggia is known by an inscription on the lower story that reads 1524. The Odeon is dated 1534 in Giuseppe Fiocco, *Alvise Cornaro: Il suo tempo e le sue opere* (Vicenza: Antoniana, 1965), p. 65; and Gunter Schweikhart, "Studien zum Werk des Giovanni Maria Falconetto," *Bolletino del Museo Civico* (Padua), 50 (1968), p. 33, n. 1. For my discussion of the Loggia and Odeon in the Cortile of Ca' Cornaro, I am indebted to the Gladys Krieble Delmas Foundation for a grant that enabled me to spend some weeks in Padua in the spring of 1977 to study and photograph the structures. At that time Paolo Carpeggiani kindly allowed me to read his thesis—published thereafter as "G. M. Falconetto, temi ed eventi di una nuova architettura civile," in *Padova, case e palazzi,* ed. L. Puppi and F. Zuliani (Vicenza: Neri Pozza, 1977), pp. 71–99—pertaining to Sebastiano Serlio's description of the Odeon and its musical function. Ludovico Zorzi discusses the Loggia and Odeon in relation to Ruzante's performance practices in "Tra Ruzzante e Vitruvio," in *Alvise Cornaro e il suo tempo,* (Padua: Antoniana, 1980), pp. 94–104, concluding that the Odeon was used for musical entertainment at a late phase in Ruzante's career, after he had stopped writing for the stage.

Figure 1.   Loggia Cornaro. Foto Lufin, Abano (Padova).

bricks, which do not retain humidity. And the four niches, because of its concave roundness, receive the voices and hold them." There, "the good gentleman had diverse jars set in place, empty ones, such as he had seen among ancient ruins."[31] Vitruvius explains that ancient architects controlled acoustics in their theaters by using bronze or clay jars proportionate to the size of the theater and set them into niches built in between the seats. The vessels are shaped so that they can pro-duce intervals of the fourth, the fifth, and so on up to

31. Sebastiano Serlio, *Tutte le opere d'architettura,* raccolte per via di considerationi da M. Gio. Domenico Scamozzi (Venice, 1584), p. 218: "Quivi si eserciteranno le musiche, et è molto al proposito per esser forma che tende alla rotondità, et tutta voltata di mattoni che non tengon punto di humido. Et li quattro nicchi per la sua rotondità concava ricevono le voci e le ritengono. . . . Il buon gentiluomo li [li fianchi] delle mura fece riempire di vasi diversi, e voti che tal cosa haveva veduta nelle rovine antiche."

Figure 2.   Odeon Cornaro. Foto Lufin, Abano (Padova).

the double octave. Whether Cornaro's sources were ar-
chaeological or philological, following ancient example
he experimented with the use of resonating jars in his
Odeon.

At the same approximate time that the Odeon was
built, a second story was added to the Loggia. This upper
story is an enclosed space with windows and a door, suitable for performances during the cold weeks of carnival.
In warmer weather spectators could sit outside in the
open courtyard on temporary movable benches ("tavole
da potersi poi levare") placed on the ground facing the
Loggia. Together, the Loggia and Odeon, indeed the
entire Cortile (courtyard) behind Ca'Cornaro, make up
a theater "ad inmitatione deli antichi" built for performances by "quel famoso Ruzante." [32] It is the first modern attempt to make a theater following ancient ex-

32. Cited in Menegazzo, "Tre scritti," p. 610; Cornaro's
self-eulogy written in the third person describes the theater.

ample. As a humanist endeavor, it refers to the plan described by Vitruvius for building theaters according to the principle of eurythmy: "beauty and fitness in the adjustments of the members."[33] As theaters require in their physical design provision for audibility and visibility, they incorporate the humanist notion that celestial harmony is audible in music and visible in architecture because of a uniform system of proportions. As a play linked to harmony practically and conceptually, *L'Anconitana* is well suited to inaugurating a space celebrating music; thus the play, like the Odeon, belongs to the years 1533–34.

The musicality of *L'Anconitana* is in its language as well as its structure. Bessa says she fell in love with Ruzante for his singing voice and Ruzante woos her anew, saying with characteristic double meaning that they would sing well together if he took the bottom part and she the top, or he would be on top if she preferred. In act 2, scene 4, Ruzante and Sier Tomao act out a contest between Ruzante's light, cheerful tunes and the Venetian's heavier, more serious songs. Such use of tonal relationships to represent personal and ethical relations becomes a familiar trope in comedies nourished by the inventions of Ruzante and his contemporaries; in *Two Gentlemen of Verona,* for example, Shakespeare has Julia advise her maid to sing the tune "Light o' Love," but Lucetta demurs, thinking her message "too heavy for so light a tune," and adding, "I bid the bass for Proteus," (I.ii) whose fickleness basely betrays Julia's love.[34]

Harmony as a model of fit proportion and a pattern for action is part of Ruzante's legacy. Compare *As You*

Hickey Morgan (New York: Dover, 1960), p. 14.

34. The edition cited here and throughout is in *The Riverside Shakespeare,* ed. G. Blakemore Evans (Boston: Houghton Mifflin, 1974).

Like It: in *L'Anconitana* there are four pairs of lovers, two aristocratic in social class and literary style and two others who complement and burlesque them. The top voices in *L'Anconitana* are spoken (in Italian) by Isotta/ Gismondo and Tancredi, reinforced by Ginevra and Teodoro; in *As You Like It* they are the voices of Rosalind and Orlando, reinforced by Celia and Oliver. Isotta in male disguise loves Tancredi and tests him; Rosalind, disguised as the male Ganymede, tests her beloved Orlando. (Both Tancredi and Orlando, incidentally, are Petrarchan poets). Isotta arranges for her sister to marry Teodoro; Rosalind arranges Celia's marriage to Oliver. Socially inferior to these poetical lovers and plainer linguistically are the rustics Ruzante and Bessa in *L'Anconitana* and, in *As You Like It,* the rustics Phebe and Silvius, who add realistic concerns and a satiric edge to their plays' many-voiced expressions of love. The bass tones in *As You Like It* are sounded by Audrey and Touchstone. Touchstone's love for Audrey, more lawful than Sier Tomao's lust for Doralice, is similarly laced with farce. Opposite to the youngest lovers just learning to temper their illusions, Tomao and Touchstone season their experience with renewed illusion; theirs are the bottom voices of a harmony in which four voices sound as one. One compares the two plays with heightened awareness not only that the Italian stage gave European Renaissance theater abundant ingredients for making comedies, but that Italian humanism also provided a theoretical foundation for theater art.

In *As You Like It* the wise shepherd Corin is content with his lot: "Sir, I am a true laborer: I earn that I eat, get that I wear, owe no man hate, envy no man's happiness, glad of other men's good, content with my harm; and the greatest of my pride is to see my ewes graze and my lambs suck" (III.ii). In *L'Anconitana* the flashback to a country world of peace and pleasure is no longer a

promise but a memory; in the *Letter to Alvarotto* it is a dream. The former clown who conducts Ruzante to the realm of Mirth asks him, in Pavano, "Do you recall ever having seen one divide into four, and four in one? Look up there, behind that fellow seated upon a chair in the gallery: to look at them they appear to be four; to hear them they seem only one."[35] Barba Polo highlights four-part harmony in his description of a mirthful world resembling Ruzante's theater. In it, the comedian fulfills the playwright-actor's conception of immortality: a life lived with an intensity that holds forever in a moment, as on the stage.

Ruzante says that the actor, like his role, is renewed with each performance; history makes a similar point about the author. Plautus, born in antiquity, is renewed in plays by Ruzante and his contemporaries, although imitation of the written word does not suffice. The texts must be brought to life in the theater, for "many things look good on paper that won't work on stage,"[36] says the Prologue to Ruzante's *Vaccaria,* speaking on Plautus's own behest. Ruzante's debt is both to authors who have wielded the pen and to acting masters like Barba Polo. He is further indebted to farmers in the Pavano, who gave his theater a voice; that voice, sometimes the actor's, sometimes the author's, varies in tone and mood from play to play, lending historical truth to his character, naturalness to his language, and lasting vitality to his theater. Music celebrates its different voices or parts

35. Ruzante, *Teatro,* p. 1235: "Te arecuòrditu mé aver vezú un solo in quatro, e quatro int'un solo? Mo véte 'l là, drio a quel che è assentò su quela cariega in balconà: a guardare i par quatro, al sentire par nomé un. Mo i ghe dise, a quelo, el Cantosona, ché se sa fare d'un solo in forma da quatro, e da quatro in forma de un solo."

36. Ruzante, *Teatro,* p. 1043: "Perché nolte cose stanno ben nella penna, che nella scena starebben male."

joined in an interactive whole. After listening to Barba Polo's commentary on Mirth, Ruzante awakes from his dream and says, "While he [Barba Polo] was saying these words I thought I heard music, whether sung or played, I know not, but of a concord or harmony I cannot express, nor would I know how to make anyone understand it unless he was sleeping, as I was."[37] Finding harmony in the natural world, Ruzante's theater projects that harmony onto society at large.

Written in a spirit of farewell, the myth of Legraçion addresses theatrical life with radiant finality, although why Beolco stopped writing after 1536 is among the unanswered questions in his career. He did, to be sure, apply to Venice in 1533 for the right to publish his two comedies that imitate Plautus, *La Vaccaria* and *La Piovana,* although none of his work appeared in print until after his death, first in incomplete editions published in Venice in 1548, 1551–52, and 1554; then in Vicenza in 1584, 1598, and 1617. The actor's legacy was inherited by comedians *dell'arte,* whose multiple voices embraced some aspects of Ruzante's *snaturalitè,* and who, like Ruzante, performed both improvised comedies and erudite plays. Ruzante was preparing to act in and probably direct *La Canace* for the Accademia degli Infiammati when he died, apparently after a brief illness, in 1542.

The playwright's legacy may be read in European comedy that builds on the theoretical humanist foundation inscribed in his plays. One compares *L'Anconitana* and *As You Like It* with heightened awareness not only of the comic ingredients they share but of the similar assumptions their playwrights make about time and

37. Ruzante, *Teatro,* p. 1243: "Mentre esso diceva queste parolle, mi parve sentire una musica, non di canti o di suoni, ma de non so che di piú concento, e di piú armonia, che non saprei darla ad intendere se non a chi dormisse, come faceva io."

place. The Italian prologue to *L'Anconitana* spoken by Time assures spectators that the hours they spend watching the play will not be subtracted from the hours of their lives; in *The Winter's Tale,* Time appears as chorus to exercise his power to advance the action by sixteen years: "I turn my glass, and give my scene such growing/ As you had slept between" (IV.i). Theatrical time and space take on a perspective natural to the spectator and his world. The action in *L'Anconitana* takes place on an urban thoroughfare, the houses occupied by Sier Tomao and Doralice overlooking a piazza with an inn visible in the distance; thus the setting assumes the kind of architectural view in perspective that was the characteristic scenic background for learned comedy. This vision of a theatrical place reflecting the spectators' world in natural perspective is well housed both in the Loggia and Odeon Cornaro, where the musical and visual values of antiquity were renewed, and in Shakespeare's Globe. *As You Like It,* the play that may have inaugurated the Globe Theater in 1599, gave that theater its motto: "All the world's a stage." On the stage of European Renaissance comedy players act out their seven ages, rehearsing in *commedia dell'arte* the parts of "the lover . . . soldier . . . the lean and slipper'd pantaloon" (II.vii), each recalling a theatrical image brought to the stage by Ruzante.

TEXT AND TRANSLATION

L'Anconitana

The Woman from Ancona

[La scena si rappresenta in Padova. Una piazza, prospiciente le case dove abitano Sier Tomao e Doralice.]

Interlocutori

TANCREDI
TEODORO } [giovani] [1]
GISMONDO

DORALICE, [cortigiana] [2]
SIER TOMAO, vechio
RUZANTE, fameglio di Tomao [3]
BESSA, fante de Doralice
GINEVRA, anconitana
GHITTA, fante di Ginevra
ISOTTA, già detta Gismondo
MENATO, vilano

[The action takes place in Padua. The houses occupied
  by Sier Tomao and by Doralice overlook a piazza.]

Speakers

TANCREDI
TEODORO   } [youths]
GISMONDO

DORALICE, [a courtesan]
SIER TOMAO, an old man
RUZANTE, a servant to Tomao
BESSA, a maidservant to Doralice
GINEVRA, a woman from Ancona
GHITTA, a maid to Ginevra
ISOTTA, first called Gismondo
MENATO, a farmer

Prologo I
[detto dal Tempo]

CHE NON PUÒ fare la cortesia de un spirito valoroso?[1]   1
Poi che sono il Tempo, vincitore di quanto è creato,
sono da la cortesia de un uomo vinto. E me, che con il
fugir mio gli anni, i mesi, [i] giorni e l'ore, etadi, seculi
e lustri consumo, e le lunghe memorie de le mortali fame
meno in preda, ha conduto nonzio di novo caso; né di
ciò mi pento, poi che a tanti nobilissimi spiriti, che quivi
veggio, son venuto a porger diletto.

Lassiate ogni altro pensiero, poi che nuovo caso amo-   2
roso siete per udire; che vi prometo, mentre che a li
piacevoli ragionamenti, che a succedere hanno, darete
udienzia, ancora che la prontezza de l'ore non possi rite-
nere, nondimeno farò che [né] per voi, né per conto del
viver vostro voleranno, ma per il rimanente del mondo sí;
e a la fine pervenuti, piú da me guadagnato che perduto
averete. E aciò di questo prendiate certa fidanza, io, in
uno di questi canti lassiato ogni mio costume, mi ponerò
a sedere fino a la fine.

Il caso è nuovo,[2] e in Padoa advenuto; dipoi a con-   3
solazione vostra ridotto, segondo l'antiquo costume, in
comedia, e a quella datto il titolo de la *Anconitana;* e son
certissimo che favola non si raconti piú bella di questa. E
udite l'argumento.

Prologue I

[spoken by Time]

Is THERE ANYTHING the courtesy of a brave spirit cannot do now that I, Time, conqueror of everything created, am conquered by a man's courtesy? Even I that in my flight consume years, months, days, and hours, ages, centuries and lustrums, and plunder the long memory of mortal fame, he has sent to herald a new event; nor do I regret it, for to the many noble spirits I see hereabout I come bringing delight.

Dismiss every other thought, for you are about to hear a new love story, and I promise you that while you listen to the entertaining speeches that follow, even though I cannot hold back the hours' hastening, nevertheless I will see to it that neither from you nor from the reckoning of your life will these hours take flight, while for the rest of the world they do; so in the end you will have gained more from me than you have lost. And to make you perfectly confident of this, I have left my habit over to the side, where I shall take my place until the end.

The story is new; it happened in Padua. Then, for your cheer, following ancient practice, it was turned into a comedy and given the title *The Woman from Ancona*. And I am very sure no better tale is told. Now hear the plot.

ARGUMENTO

Tancredi e Teodoro, gioveni siciliani, e Isota, donna di   4
Gagieta, che soto abito di uomo si fa chiamare Gismondo, furno presi tuta tre da corsali, e venduti ad un
Moro; dipoi da un mercatante veneziano riscatati e con-
doti a Vineggia, con promessa di non mai da lui partirsi,
se intieramente non era da loro de' suoi denari sodisfato, i quali aveano in Sicilia mandati a togliere. E perché
erano tuta tre di virtú gentilissime vestiti, venero in
questa città, fatti suoi avisi, a conciarse, per mezo de la
virtú loro, a' servigii di alcuna valorosa donna, da quella
traendo li denari per sodisfare al mercatante. E mentre
questi tre giovani racontano le virtú sue ad una cortigiana, chiamata Doralice, che ad una finestra dimorava,   5
avene che una bellissima donna veneziana, moglie de
uno richissimo vechio similmente veniziano, già sensale
stato, chiamato sier Tomao, inamorassi di questo Gismondo, credendolo uomo, e induce il vechio marito
suo a riscuoterlo. Il quale, amando sconciamente Doralice, mentre che per mezo de un suo fameglio, detto
Ruzante, che altresí in una fante de Doralice ferventemente è inamorato, cerca di venire a l'ultimo amoroso
diletto, aviene che Ginevra, donna vedoa anconitana,
veduto Gismondo in Ancona, e falsamente credendolo
uomo, del suo amore ardentissimamente presa, con una
sua sola fante, Ghitta chiamata, in abito di uomo am-   6
bedua sonno venute in questa città per ritrovarlo; dapo'
longhi ragionamenti e accidenti amorosi, viene a ritro-
vare quella essere una sua sorella, otto anni peregrina andata, e da lei per morta pianta. Ultimamente si maritano:
Isota prende per isposo Tancredi, e Ginevra Teodoro,
trati di servitú da certi gentiluomeni padoani; e a godersi
tornano ne la loro patria. Sier Tomao e il fameglio suo
Ruzante ordina con Doralice e Bessa sua fante il modo

PLOT

Two Sicilian youths named Tancredi and Teodoro, and Isotta, a girl from Gaeta dressed like a man and going by the name Gismondo, were captured by pirates, who sold them to a Moor; then they were ransomed by a Venetian merchant, who took them to Venice on their promise that they would never abandon him without repaying his money in full, and they have sent to Sicily for the payment. Meanwhile, because all three of them are clothed in gentle arts, they have come to this city, knowing its reputation, to seek employment for their talents in the service of some virtuous lady from whom they might earn money to repay the merchant.

While these three youths recount their talents to a courtesan named Doralice, whom they find tarrying at her window, an attractive Venetian woman, the wife of a wealthy old Venetian gentleman, falls in love with Gismondo (who she thinks is a man), and she persuades her husband to pay his ransom. Her husband has taken a lewd liking to Doralice and, with the help of his manservant, Ruzante, who's just as madly in love with Doralice's maid, is trying to reach love's consummate pleasure.

Ginevra, a widow from Ancona, who had seen Gismondo in Ancona, mistaken him for a man, and fallen ardently in love, has come to this city to find him, accompanied by a single maidservant, a girl named Ghitta, both of them disguised as men. After much discussion and love's surprises, Ginevra discovers that Gismondo is her sister, who had gone abroad eight years earlier and whom she had mourned for dead. In the end they are married: Isotta takes Tancredi for her husband and Ginevra marries Teodoro, all of them released from their bondage by some Paduan gentlemen, and they return to

35

di godersi questa sera insiemme; vano ad una villa non guari lontana.

Ma parmi udire che quello che in breve parole vi ho   7
divisato, essi si aconciano con longo ordine e con piú piacevoli parole [a raccontarvi]. Onde, se vago desio de novelle cosse vi muove ponto l'animo, a le sue parole date benigna atenzione.

their homeland to live happily ever after. Sier Tomao and his familiar, Ruzante, arrange with Doralice and her maidservant, Bessa, to enjoy this night together; they're going to a villa not far from here.

But I think I hear that what I have sketched in a few words they are ready to perform at length and more enjoyably. So if a longing for something new stirs your spirit, give their words your kind attention.

Prologo II

[detto da Ruzante[1]]

Perché g'intrighi d'assé fate e i schiapuçi del mondo in purassé vie e muò el çelibrio e le fantasie de gi uomeni va volzanto e revolzanto e sbragagnanto; e perzòntena el se ve' che uno ha piasere de andar co le biestie e deventa boaro, un altro vacaro, un altro pegoraro; un altro arà piasere de laorar in campagna, un altro de essere massaro de ca' e de smassarizare, quel'altro de guagnar roba, quel'altro de costionizare e farse braoso. E l'altro, che sarà stò sbolzonò d'Amore, no zarlerà mé d'altro, e se penserà sempre mé a che muò el porae menar via la so morosa, e cognosse le morose de tuti, e tuti quigi che è inamorè; ora el sta de buona vuogia, ora de mala, ora el sgnica, ora el se la ri'. E de quisti inamorè ghe n'è pí che ne gh'è çéleghe al tempo d'i migi.   1

E perzòntena mo mi, che a' son mi mo, e che a' sè quelo che se pò saere, de Amore a' vuogio rengare, e no de altro; e chive, chialò, quençena, chialòndena, chivelò, chí in sto luogo, a' ve vuogio far sentire [cossí bel] straparlamento de Amore, con se sentisse mé, intravegnú chí in Pava; che adesso chí, con a' saí, e' no gh'è se no çielo e amore, e chi no è inamorò e chi favela d'altro, la no ghe buta bianco.   2

A' gh'he intendú fremamen che Amore, per paura de' Turchi, ch'i no l'impalesse adesso in ste moeste, è partú de Çipro,[2] da ca' so, elo e so mare, e sí è vegnú a ficarse in ste muragie, per esser a la segura e in luogo pí forte, e fa inamorare tuti. Mo no viu che chi no è duniarin e inamorò, e che no vaghe con el regazo e con la muleta   3

38

Prologue II

[spoken by Ruzante]

PLOTS OF EVERY SORT and the world's stumbling blocks
in different ways and means twist and turn and overturn
human wit and fancy, so we see that one man likes to
herd cattle, and he becomes a cattleman; another a cow-
herd, another a shepherd; another likes to labor in the
country, another to manage a household and farms; still
another likes to acquire goods, and another to fight and
bully. Then some fellow is smitten by Love. He speaks
of nothing else and he's always figuring out some way to
run off with his sweetheart. He knows who's beloved
and who are the lovers. Sometimes he's in a good mood,
sometimes bad; now he weeps, now he starts laughing.
And there are more of these lovers around than sparrows
in millet season.

And that's why I, yes I, knowing all there is to know,
I want to talk about Love, and nothing else; here, right
here, over here, here indeed, right here, on this very
spot. And I want you to listen to the [best] Love story
anyone has ever heard, and it happened right here in
Padua, where now, as you know, there is nothing beneath the sky but a world all of love, and anyone who's
not in love or who speaks of anything else is out of place.

I've heard for a fact that Love, fearing the Turks might
impale him during one of their war maneuvers, has left
his home in Cyprus, he and his mother, and he's come
poking himself inside these city walls so he'll be safe inside a strong place; and he's making everyone fall in love.
Don't you see that everyone teases any man who's not

dunianto, tuti el trogna? Mo no viu che le done che n'è cortesarine, i dise che le n'è bele? Mo chi cancaro[3] favelerae d'altro? E tanto pí che se no foesse Amore; vache, piegore, scrove, cavale, né altra biestia del roverso mondo[4] farae mé furto.

Amore, an? Puh! mo a vivessam deboto, se no foesse 4 Amore. Mo no se fícalo, per farghe vivere, chiamentre in la tera? Chi se ghe ficherae, se no elo, a inamorar la tera, per norigar le biave? A' murissàn pur da fame. Amore, an? [El no sa andare in gi arbori, no l'ha el tirò a fargi far furto? Amore, an?] Mo guardè se l'è omo da ben, sto Amore, e si el ne vol ben, e si l'è de descrizion: perché el cognosse che con l'entra in gi arbore, el g'inamora, e perché i stropari, con gi è inamorè, le strope no tien, che le n'è bone, e per no ghe far sto dano, el sta tanto a intrarghe, che da quel tempo aón rivò de bruscare, e no aón pí besogno de strope.

Amore, an? No favelare d'Amore, che 'l povereto, per 5 amor nostro, e per farghe comelitè al magnare, se fica soto aqua, a far inamorar i pesse e fargi smultiplicarc. Chi fa andar le anguile in frega? Solamen Amore. Amore, an? Mo per farghe piasere, no falo vegnire i rosignuoli a inamorarse in sto paese, che i sona sí bon a cantare, che se perderae Agnoli, Arcagnoli, Guanzelista, Martore, Confessore, Mare Biata? Amore, an? Andassàn a scazafasso, no favelare mé d'altro e no voler ben a altro.

Mi inchín damò a' son sí inamorò in Amore, che ghe 6 farae cossí vontiera un servissio, con cossa che a' faesse mé.[5] Mo se no foesse Amore, no sessen vivi, né negun mé nassú? Mo a' cherzo ben de no, ché Amore, con dise la leza, fa marío e mogiere de du uno, che la dise: «Erunt duo in carne l'una».[6] Ché, se 'l marío foesse d'una volontè e la mogier d'un'altra, e uno se voltasse in qua e l'altro in là, e' nassessan in le neghe! Mo l'Amore se caza de mezo, e fa de du uno, e a quel muò se ven a impolare e nassire. Mo no sa tuto omo, che incalma, s'te sè, un

attentive to women and in love, or doesn't go courting with a pageboy and a mule. Don't you see that if a woman's not a courtesan, they say she isn't beautiful? Who the devil talks about anything else? All the more so since if it weren't for Love neither cows, nor sheep, nor sows, nor mares, nor any other creature in the whole upside-down world would ever be fruitful.

Love? Pooh! We wouldn't be alive at all if it weren't for Love. Doesn't he poke his way down into the earth to bring us life? Who else would plunge in to fill the earth with love and nourish the crops? Otherwise we'd die of hunger. Love? [Can't he enter trees to make them fruitful? Love?] Isn't he a good fellow, this Love, doesn't he love us, isn't he prudent: knowing that when he enters the trees he fills them with love, but that when willows are in love their shoots don't hold, they're useless, so to spare us damage he waits to enter them until after we've finished pruning and we no longer need osiers.

Love? Don't talk about Love. That poor boy, for love of us and to make food plentiful, plunges underwater to make the fish fall in love and multiply. Who makes eels spawn? Only Love. Love? For our pleasure, doesn't he bring nightingales here to fall in love—whose song would outsing the song of angels, archangels, evangelists, martyrs, confessors, the Blessed Mother? Love? We'd go to pieces if we talked about anything else or loved any other.

As for me, I'm so in love with Love that I'd gladly do him a service I've never done anyone. If it weren't for Love would we be alive or would anyone be born? I think not, for Love, the Law says, makes husband and wife from two into one. As it says: "And they were both of one flesh." Because if the husband leaned one way and the wife another, and one turned this way and the other that, we'd be born at the buttocks! But Love plunges in the middle and makes two into one, and

41

arbore, e sia pur vivo e fresco, se 'l vò, se 'l calmo e 'l
calmeto n'è inamorè, el no se arpigerave mé? Poh, l'è un
gran fato!

Amore, an? Amore no se sa ficarc int'i puti e int'i   7
uomeni gruossi [de] çelibrio? Con sarae che, con un putato boaruolo sente amore, de fato el vol vestirse da festa?
Amore, an? No, l'amore no fa deventar balarini? No, l'ha
ferdo. El no sa far deventar saltarini e gaiardini? No, l'ha
mosche. El no sa far deventar cantarini? No, el trogna.
El no sa far deventar spadaçini? No, l'ha paura. Amore,
an? Mo chi cancaro sarae quel cancaro de quelú, che vo-
lesse mé favelare d'altro ca d'amore?

Amore per mar e per tera! Per amore de vu, bela brigà,   8
e per farve cossa che ve sea in piasere, a' fazón sta co-
mieria, che è tuta çielo e amore. E per amore che 'l ghe
n'è de quigi sletràn che dise che comidiare vol dir magnare[7] (azò che a' no intendessè per sta via, che sarae ben
el cancaro), Amore, per amore me, ve priega che aspitè
che a' rivón questa, ch'a' ne farón un'altra. E mi, an mi
per amor de Amore, a' ve priego, brigà, che per so
amore, azò che chi sente d'amore no se desnamore,
quigi che no va in amore, se inamore. E perché el po-
verom d'Amore sí è con ièrinu nu, quando muzàvimo
per i Toíschi e per i Spagnaruoli,[8] l'è muzò an elo da ca'
so, per amore de no essere impalò. E perzòntena a' ve
priego che a' no 'l vogiè refuare da tegnirlo infra vu,
femene e uomeni, a bel fato tuti, perché 'l dà piasere,
elo, do' 'l se fica; e con a' v'he dito de sora, se 'l no foesse
elo, da che sassàngie al mondo? E tamentre vu, femene,
che a' no sassè cognossú.

Mi, a' vuò dir de mi, se foesse una femena, vegnisse   9
pur Amore da ora, da strasora, a' l'albergherae sempre
ontiera. Questa è la veritè; ché, inanzo che cognossesse
Amore, an mi, perché aéa aldío dire che 'l iera ria cossa,
a' me 'l çercava da parar da çerca da mia posta. E a' ve
dirè an pí: co' me sentía muovere l'amore, de fato tolea

that's how we are conceived and born. Doesn't everyone who's ever grafted a tree know that even though the tree may be quick and fresh, if the stock and the scion don't fall in love they won't take hold? Poh, it's true!

Love? Doesn't Love get into stripling youths as well as mature men? How come when a young stable boy feels love, he suddenly wants to deck himself out for a holiday? Love? Doesn't Love make us dancers? No, he's leaden. Does he make us leapers and tumblers? No, he's prim. Does he make us singers? No, he laughs at the thought. Can he make swordsmen of us? No, he's afraid. Love? Who the devil would that devil be who ever wanted to speak of anything but Love?

Love by land and by sea! And for love of you, fair company, and for your pleasure, we present this comedy, which is everything beneath the sky that is love. And for love of those scholars who say that comedy is comestible (so long as you don't think so, for that would be a devil of a mess) Love, for love of me, asks you to stay until this play is over; then we'll perform another. And I, I for love of Love, pray you, folks, for love of him not to let anyone in love fall out of love, and whoever is not in love, let him fall in love. And because that poor wretch Love is like us when we were fleeing from Germans and Spaniards, he too has fled his home for love of not being impaled. Therefore I pray you not to refuse to take him among you, ladies and gentlemen, all of you, because he gives pleasure, that fellow, wherever he pokes in; and as I've already said, if it weren't for him, how would we come into the world? And you women, you especially would be ignored.

As for my own self, if I were female, were Love to come at the right time or ahead of time, I would always lodge him gladly. The truth is that before I knew Love I'd always heard he was something terrible, so I tried to handle him my own way. And I'll tell you something

l'ordegno in man, e sí me spuava su i palmuzi de le man,
e man mena e laora tanto a zapare, a vangare e sbailare,
infin de tanto che 'l povereto arbassava el cao e andasea
in là, e no me dasea pí fastidio. Mo dasché a' la proviè la
prima fià, a' ve dighe che a' he abú de gran piasere da
elo, che pensàntomelo, a' no posso star ch'a' no spue.
[*Sputa*].

E da tanto ben ch'a' ghe vuogio, a' m'he sí incatigiò   10
el çelibrio e la smalmuoria, che a' no sè quel che a' iera
vegnú a far chivelò. Ben, an, de davera: mo el vignerà
tri, tri, tri, e po un che ha lome quatro, e po du altri, e sí
sarà inamorè. Oh, cancaro i magne, mo la serà pur la bela
filatuoria, la bela novela; e quelú che favelerà a ela, e po
un che no ghe serà mé pí stò, vegnirà an elo; e po, con
l'averà dito e dito, el vegnerà po un altro. O cancaro, la
sarà la bela cancaro de novela!

Tasí pure, a' i vuò andare a ciamare. Tasí pure, mostrè   11
che no abiè intendú zò che vi abia dito, ché i se score-
zarave. Tasí pure. Aldí, a' sento ch'i vien mo a dire. [*Fa
cenno di ascoltare ed esce*].

else: when I felt love stir, I quickly grabbed my tool in my hand, spit on the palms of my hands, and down I pulled and I went to work hoeing, digging, spading, until the poor creature lowered its head and went away and troubled me no more. But then when I tried it for the first time, believe me, I had such a good time with it that thinking about it I have to spit. [*He spits*].

And I love him so much he has so confounded my brain and my memory that I forget why I'm here. Oh yes, that's right: now some characters will appear—one, two, three, then a fourth, then two more—and they'll all be in love. Damn them, it's a fine yarn, a new tale; a man will speak with a woman, then someone we haven't seen before will arrive, and after he has said and done, another. Damn, it's a hell of a good tale!

Quiet now, I'll call them. Quiet please, pretend you didn't hear what I said or they'll lose heart. Quiet please. Listen, I hear them coming. [*He gestures to listen and exits*].

ATTO PRIMO

SCENA PRIMA

Tancredi, Teodoro, Gismondo, poi Doralice

TANCREDI. Io non ci veggio altro modo a liberarci, che 1
el mezo delle virtú nostre. Elle sonno di sorte che deveno piacere a tute le donne, e maggiormente alle donne di questa famosa cità; le quali, secondo che ho udito ragionare, oltra che sono cortesi e bellissime, sono ancora amanti delle virtú, e di le persone in cui fiorisse essa virtú. Facilmente potrà cadere ne l'animo di queste madonne voler imparar de queste nostre scienzie, e per riscato di noi darano al mercatante quello che elgi diede per noi al Moro.

Lo esser lontano da le case nostre ci concederà senza 2
alcuna vergogna andar visitando le altrui, e alle gentildonne di quelle far le virtú nostre chiare, et a loro adiuto adimandare, e seco stare a' suoi servigii, fino che o letre o denari da la patria nostra veranno. E se per tuto ciò avenisse che mai non venissero, a quali piú degne, a quali piú benigne persone potremo esser sugietti, che a queste nobilissime madonne? Io per me piú cara mi terrei tal servitú, che altra libertà.

TEODORO. Veramente et io altresí sonno del tuo pa- 3
rere, e se mi credesse di divenire il maggiore signore del mondo, non gabarei il mercatante; il quale, oltre che per riscato di noi, che eravamo schiavi, pagò quella quantità di moneta, ci ha datto ancora libertà, che ove piú ne piace andiamo, per ritrovar modo di rendergli li sui denari; che è stata gran cortesia, senza voler esser sicuro.

GISMONDO. Non faciamo queste ragioni adesso, quello 4
che abiamo comminciato seguiamo. E tu, Tancredi, saluta quella gentildonna, che a quella finestra dimora [*accenna a Doralice*], e a lei dippoi racontiamo il caso nostro

ACT ONE

SCENE ONE

TANCREDI, TEODORO, GISMONDO, then DORALICE

TANCREDI. I see no other way for us to gain our freedom than by putting our talents to use. They are the
kind that should please all women, especially the ladies
of this renowned city who are, as I have heard, not only
courteous and very beautiful, but also lovers of virtuous
accomplishments and of persons in whom these virtues
flower. It may well strike the fancy of these ladies to want
to learn about our accomplishments, and then for our
ransom they will give the merchant the sum he paid for
us to the Moor.

Because we are far from home we may approach
strangers' homes unashamed to explain our talents to the
ladies of the house, ask for their help, and remain in their
service until letters or money arrive from our homeland.
And in the event these never arrive, to what worthier,
kindlier persons could we be subject than to these very
noble ladies? For my part, I would hold such servitude
dearer than some other freedom.

TEODORO. In truth, I am of your same opinion; and
even if I thought I could become the grandest gentleman
in the world, I would not deceive the merchant: not
only did he pay a large sum of money for our ransom
when we were slaves, he gave us liberty to go wherever
we like so we can find a way to return his money. He
showed great courtesy by not requiring any security.

GISMONDO. Let's not discuss this now; let us continue
what we have begun. You, Tancredi, greet that gentlewoman who is resting at that window. [*He points to
Doralice*]. Let us tell her of our plight and describe our

e le virtú nostre. Forse, se ella non ne aiuterà, ne prove-
derà de aiuto per altra via.

TANCREDI. Ben hai detto, Gismondo. [*Con un inchino*   5
saluta Doralice] Ben possa star Vostra Signoria, nobillissima madonna.

DORALICE. [*alla finestra*] Siate ben venuti, gentiluomeni.

TANCREDI. Nobillissima madonna, nui fummo presi   6
da certi corsali sopra una nave di nostre mercantancie
carica, e dippoi venduti ad un famoso Moro, sotto la po-
testà del quale, fra molti disaggi, aspra vita finora abiam
menata; ogni speranza lassando non mai di tal servitú
ussire, se non sopravenia uno mercatante veniziano, il
qualle, cognossuti noi per cristiani, per riscato nostro
diede certa quantità di moneta al Moro, a cui eravamo
stati venduti, e noi seco fin a Vinegia trasse, con promessa nostra fàtali mai non si dover partir da lui, se intieramente de li suoi denari non era da noi sodisfato. E   7
perché ci ritroviamo lontani da la patria nostra, che è
Sicilia, ove con letere a' parenti nostri ne abiamo avisato,
ma perché per la longheza del viagio aviene talora che si
sogliono smarire le letere, abiamo fra noi istessi delibe-
rato metersi a' servigii di alcuna nobillissima madonna,
et ella per noi pagando li denari al mercatante, che per
riscato di noi spendeno, a lui in un medesimo tratto e a
noi e alla gentildonna sodisfare: a lui, che di suoi denari
non patirà longo disaggio, a noi che de l'obrigo che con
esso abiamo ci libereremo, a la cortese donna poi in che
sodisfaremo intendereti.

E prima da me incomminciando, dico quella gentil   8
madonna per la cui cortesia di cossí fatto obrigo sarò
tratto, oltre che ad un piciol ceno, in tute le cosse che
piacer li fieno, me avrà pronto, e oltre che potrà lodarsi
di un parangon di fideltà, di alcuna particular virtú potrà
servirsi di me, e questa è che io ne la mia gioveneza disposi li mei primi pensieri a la dolceza d'i versi de la vol-

accomplishments. If she does not help us herself, perhaps she'll provide help in some other way.

TANCREDI. Well said, Gismondo. [*He greets Doralice with a bow*]. Rest you well, Your Ladyship, most noble madam.

DORALICE. [*at her window*] Welcome, gentlemen.

TANCREDI. Noble lady, we were captured by corsairs from aboard a ship laden with our own goods, then sold to a famous Moor in whose power, amid many discomforts, we have led a hard life until now. We had given up hope of escaping from that servitude when a Venetian merchant appeared and, seeing that we were Christians, he paid the Moor a large sum of money for our ransom and took us with him to Venice on our pledge that we would never abandon him without repaying his money in full. We find ourselves far from our homeland in Sicily, where we have informed our relatives of this matter by letter; but because the journey is long and letters are likely to go astray, we have decided to enter the service of some noble lady, who by repaying the merchant the money he spent for our ransom will at once satisfy him and us and herself: him, because he will not be inconvenienced of his money for long; us, because we will be released from our obligation; and how we will satisfy the gentle lady, you shall hear.

Beginning first with myself, I say that the gentlewoman by whose courtesy I shall be discharged of my obligation, besides having me ready at her call to do her every pleasure, and besides commending to herself a paragon of fidelity, she will have at her service a special virtue of mine: that in my youth I applied my first thoughts to the sweetness of poetry in the vernacular. I shall take it upon myself, therefore, for so long as I live,

gar lingua. Me obrigherò adonque, fino che mi basterà   9
la vita, consacrare al bel nome suo li pensieri, l'ingegno,
la lingua, la mano, el stille. E quella con ogni mio studio
mi sforzerò di fare risonare fra li nobeli inteletti, tessendo
in rime ellette e con amorose lode dipingendo or li occhi
suoi leggiadri, or le bionde trecie, or l'onesto petto, or
la bianca mano, or li cari sguardi, le parole, gli atti, la
leggiadria, la onestate, l'abito, l'andare; e in diverse composizioni, in capitoli, in epistole, in egloghe, in canzoni,
in sestine, in soneti, in madriali, in stance, in ode, in bar-
zelette, in balate. E veramente non piciola offerta a l'al-
tezza de l'animo di qualunque donna deve essere questa
mia, né poco cara, pensando quanto grande siano le
force della pena. Le force de la pena sono troppo maggiori che coloro non istimano, che quelle con conossi-
mento provate non hanno.[1] Veramente io direi cossí fate
cosse in lode di una bella donna, che non che a sé stessa
piacendo si teniria cara, ma dal mondo tutto saria tenuta
cara e apregiata; e cosí del contrario direi cose, che,
udendole, non potendo morire, li faria venir in odio la
vitta e dal mondo altressí esser odiata.

Né crediate, per tuto ciò che ho detto, che di tanta   10
prosonzione sia, che poeta mi voglie dire; ma amante di
essa poesia mi dirò ben, e bene o male che mi dica, lascio
nel benigno iudizio di quelle persone, che piú di me
sanno. Voi dunque, i miei compagni, il cominciato ra-
gionamento sequendo, a questa gentil signora li nostri
intendimenti fareti noti, et ella, intendendo le virtú nostre, per lei segliendo il piú confacevole a sue bisogna, li
altri dui a vicine, o amiche, o parente servendo, potrà far
liberare.

DORALICE. Veramente gentillissima virtú è questa vos-   11
tra, e poche donne o niuna è che se ne facia conto. Da
che siamo noi, levàtane via questa poca bellezza, la qual
pochi anni guastano? Da nulla. Onde che un scritore ne
faria sempre rimaner belle, doppo morte ancora. Vardate

to consecrate to her good name my thoughts, wit, language, hand, and style. And I will strive with all diligence to make her name resound among noble minds, weaving choice rhymes and painting with loving praise her bright eyes, her blond tresses, her chaste breast, her white hand, her cherished glances, her words, actions, grace, virtue, dress, and gait; in various compositions, in *capitoli,* epistles, eclogues, canzones, sestinas, sonnets, madrigals, stanzas, odes, witty songs, and ballads. Mine is not a small offer to the high spirit of some woman nor of little value, considering how great is the power of the pen. The power of the pen is far greater than anyone imagines who has not learned it from experience. Faith, I would say such things in praise of a beautiful woman that by liking them, not only would she think well of herself, she would be valued and esteemed by the whole world; just as I could say things to the contrary that, if she heard them, unable to die, she would come to hate life and be hated in turn by the world.

Nor should you think for all I have said that I am so presumptuous as to call myself a poet; rather, I claim to be a lover of poetry, and whether I am right or wrong I leave to the good judgment of those who know best. Now then, you, my companions, pursuing the course I have begun, make our intentions known to this gentle lady so that she, when she has learned our virtues and chosen the one most suited to her needs, by placing the other two in the service of neighbors or friends or relatives, will be able to set them free.

DORALICE. Very noble indeed is this ability of yours, and there are few women, if any, who appreciate it. What is left of us when we are deprived of our slight beauty, which a few years wither away? Nothing. While

che è avenuto di Madonna Laura, tanto lodata dal Petrarca:[2] che si trovano al dí d'oggi de quelli, che, infiammati de la sua bellezza, ancor sospirano e si dogliono non
esser stati al suo tempo, overo che ella non sia stata al
nostro. Gran forza hanno e' versi.

Orsú, e di questo altro giovene qual virtú è la sua?
Ditte, di grazia.

TEODORO. Allo incontro de l'oro, che quella cortese   12
anima di qualunque valorosa madonna spenderà per ri-
scuotermi, sarò sempre a quella cordialissimo servitore.
E perché comun desio è de ciascuna donna, anci dirò
somma cura, di acressere le sue bellezze naturale, e in ciò
e tempo e danari ispendeno in mille maniere, in aque
incorporate con sulimato, in belletti cotti, in chiarimenti, in lustri, in bianchigiamenti di capelli, in sotiglia-
menti di peli, in colorimenti di carne, e in mille altre
brute onture; le quali cosse, quanto piú per piciol spazio
di tempo vi faciano parere a gli ochi di coloro che vi
mirano belle e riguardevoli, tanto piú quanto cominciate
a discendere alle tepida etade, vi mostrano soze e brute;
perciò che, mancata nel vostro viso la prima virtú de'
belleti, de' lustri, de' chiarimenti, che piú vaghe e piú
colorite a gli uomeni vi facea vedere, rimane nelle delicate carne vostre la sua fecia, ch'è possente di mutar la
lor morbida natura nella sua ruvida qualità. E quindi na-   13
scono le spesse crespe, che per la fronte, per le guancie,
per il petto inanci alla debita etade apaiono; quindi di-
vengono rari e canuti e' capelli, quindi il palido colore,
quindi si infrigidiscono e cadeno i denti inanci tempo,
quindi li ochi par che continuamente lagrimano, quasi la
lor presta perduta leggiadria piangendo; senza che le labra de' mariti vostri, che al volto per basciarvi vi si aco-
stano, ne ritornano spesse volte invescate, e aviene che
men belle parete, quanto piú con questi imbratamenti vi
cercate de abellire.

Ma quella, alli cui servigii sarò, non averà di questi   14

a writer would make us beautiful forever, even after death. See what has become of Madonna Laura, so praised by Petrarch that even today there are men inflamed by her beauty, who still sigh and regret not having lived in her time or she in ours. Great is the power of verse.

Come now, this other youth, what is his accomplishment? Pray, tell.

TEODORO. In exchange for the gold, which the gentle spirit of some worthy lady will spend to ransom me, I will forever be her most welcome servant because it is the common desire of all women, indeed their utmost concern, to augment their natural beauty, to which effect they spend time and money in a thousand ways, on waters mixed with distillates, on cosmetics, cleansers, polishes, bleaches for hair, skin smoothers, tints, and on a thousand other foul unguents which, for the brief span of time they may make you appear beautiful and remarkable in the eyes of your admirers, so much more when you begin your declining years do they show you vile and ugly; because when your face has lost the first blush of the cosmetics, polishes, and brighteners that make you look lovelier and rosier to men, a residue remains on your delicate skin capable of changing its quality into a coarse condition. Then thick wrinkles appear before their time on your brow, your cheeks, and your breast; then your hair turns thin and gray; thence your pallor; your teeth loosen and fall out prematurely; your eyes seem to water continually as if weeping for their lost brightness, not to mention that your husbands' lips, drawing near your face to kiss you, many times withdraw soiled, so you seem less beautiful the more you try to beautify yourselves with this trash.

But the woman I serve will have none of these poul-

empiastri, né onguenti, ma pure aque senza corpo, di semplici erbe stilate a' fochi di odorifere legna; la virtú delle quali non solamente in abellire il viso, il petto e 'l colo valerà, ma rempierà le carne de' piú soavi odori che in excellenzia sieno. Aqua da crespare e biondeggiare le trecie, aqua da allargare e serenar la fronte, aqua da inarcare et imbrunir le ciglia, aqua da colorire le guanzie, aqua da arossir le labra, aqua da far li denti bianchi, aqua da far la gola bianca, aqua da far morbido il petto, aqua da far bianche le mani; la virtú delle quali, nel loco dove sarano adoperate, durerà per tre giorni et altre tante notte, e non averà di loro como di questi volgari belleti aviene, che quando la matina vi levate, vi lasciano nel viso e sotto li ochi e nella carne una certa palideza, di mille várii colori adombrata.

Imaginase adonque quella leggiadra donna, a cui 15 serò servitore, quanto da l'altre sarà istimata excellente, quanta virtú aquistarà con piciola quantità di moneta. Oltra di questo, di odori, di perfumi potrà tutte le altre donne di gran lunga avanzare, perché io toglio l'odore al muschio, al zibeto, a l'ambra, al bengioí, al spico, al storace, a cui piú, a cui meno; e di quelli compono una mistura, mescolando con essa alcuni semi di erba, alcuni fiori, che diventa di tanta soavità, che per ferma opinione tengo che a l'odor di quella si potria l'alma e il corpo insiemmemente nutrire. Le aque rose, le aque di gesamini, le aque di fior di melangoli, le aque di profumo, le aque nanfe, le aque di fior di cedri per nulla le reputo, perché io stillerò aque di non conosciute erbe, né mai a notizia de altro uomo pervenute che alla mia, che vincerano de odore li piú mirabili, che oggi siano in precio.

Porgete ora orechie alle virtú di questo altro compagno, che de un'altra guisa de virtú è dottato.

DORALICE. O galante virtú! Sí, per mia fe', ma voglio 16 pur in questa parte deffender le donne. Quelle che si fanno belle, se sonno maritate, lo fanno per piacere alli

tices or unguents; rather, pure waters distilled from plain herbs over the flames of fragrant wood; their efficacy will not only act to beautify her face, her breast, and her neck, but will permeate her skin with the sweetest odors most excellent. Water to curl her locks and make them golden, water to broaden and smooth her forehead, water to arch and shadow her eyebrows, to color her cheeks, redden her lips, make her teeth sparkle, whiten her throat, firm her breast, and whiten her hands: and wherever they are applied their efficacy will last for three days and as many nights; nor will they perform like common cosmetics that when you wake up in the morning leave on your face, under your eyes, and on your skin a pallor shaded with a thousand different hues.

Imagine, then, that fair lady whose servant I shall be, how superior other women will deem her, how much skill she will purchase for so little coin. Morever, her fragrances and perfumes will far surpass those of all other women, because I take the odor of musk, civet, ambergris, benzoin, lavender, and storax, some more, some less, and I compose a mixture of these, blending with it some herbal seeds and blossoms until it becomes so sweet that I firmly believe its essence nourishes both body and soul. Rosewater, jasmine, orange, perfume essence, orange-flower water, and essence of lemon blossom I count for naught, because I distill essences from unknown herbs that have never come to anyone's attention but mine, and they will vanquish the most marvelous scents prized today.

Now lend your ear to the accomplishments of this other companion, who has been dowered with gifts of another sort.

DORALICE. O gallant art! Yes, by my faith; yet I will defend women in this matter. Those who beautify themselves, if they are married, do it to please their hus-

mariti loro, aciò non si svoglino di loro e vadino a l'altrui femine. Né per tuto ciò non li possono far rimanere, che non le lassino sole e frede la notte ne' leti loro, e vadino altrove procaciandosi di novo cibo. Ma lassiamo queste parole. E questo altro giovene di che altra virtú è dottato?

GISMONDO. Non posso, gentilissima madonna, [fare], in [quello] che servirò quella magnifica madonna, per la cui generosità sarò rescatato, ch'io non dica che il padre mio doi figliuoli ebbe, senza piú; et egli e la madre, noi d'un medesmo parto avendo partoriti, passo[rno] di questa vita. Per il che da uno avo materno nostro fummo fina alli sete anni alevati; dippoi, per odio di nostri parenti a noi portato, e per fugire le insidie loro a noi nella vita tese, fummo disgionti. Quello che di mio fratello avenisse, non potei mai risapere; io, in abito di donna, fino alli diciotto anni stei rinchiuso in uno monasterio de monache, ove, in cambio delle letere, a l'acco, alla roca, al fuso diedi opera. E prima imparai a tirare in filo el lino e la lana, dippoi a comporre e tessere le telle, e dippoi con l'acco di sette di varii colori trapongerle, e ricamarle d'oro e di argento, e in quelle depingere e colorire figure d'omeni, d'animali, d'arbori, di paesi lontani, di fontane [e] boschi; e in breve quello che faria un penello de un dotto dipintore, io con l'acco, con la seda tinta de varii colori farò. 17

E ciò che per me si dipinge è con atti, con movenzie, con gerature, con panni, ignudi, in maiestà, in perfilo, in corzio, adumbrati e coloriti con reflexi, con ombre morte; e se de diece mille figure le piú belle parte scegliesse, quelle scio benissimo acompagnare (il che in pochi si ritrova), e dippoi colorire di azuro, di giallo, di perso, di vermiglio, e piú e meno, come rechiede lo effetto della figura. 18

Li lavori di camise e di gorgiere, di traponti aurati e serici, benissimo li scio fare. Oltre di ciò, ho perfetissimo 19

bands so they won't lose interest in them and chase after other men's women. Nor for all that can they keep them at home and prevent their leaving them alone and cold at night while they go elsewhere to dine. But enough. This other youth, what is his skill?

GISMONDO. I cannot, most kind lady, say how I will serve that munificent lady by whose generosity I shall be ransomed without explaining that my father had two children and no others; then he and my mother, who gave birth to the two of us at the same delivery, passed on from this life. We were raised by our mother's father until we were seven years old; then because of hatred borne against us by our relatives, we were separated. What happened to my brother, I was never able to find out. As for myself, dressed like a girl, I was confined until my eighteenth year in a monastery of nuns, where I applied myself not to letters but to the needle, the distaff, and the spindle. First, I learned to spin flax and wool into thread, then to compose and weave cloth, and then to sew the cloth with a needle and thread of multicolored silk, embroider it with gold and silver, and draw and color figures of men, animals, trees, distant landscapes, fountains, and woods; in short, what a skilled painter would do with a brush I do with a needle and silk dyed many colors.

The figures I depict are done with gesture, movement, torsion; clothed, nude, in majesty, in profile, in perspective, shaded and colored with reflections or in shadow; and if you were to select the most beautiful parts of ten thousand figures, I would know very well how to assemble them (which few artists do), and then color them blue, yellow, purple, vermilion, more or less, as the effect of the figure requires.

I am skilled at making chemises and ruffs, golden and silk embroideries. Moreover, I have excellent taste and I

iudizio e intiera cognizione di adornare una donna di
vestimenti, di scufie, di balci, di trecie, di gorgierie; e
scio qualli colori di drapi sieno piú confaceveli alla
donna bianca e qualli alla bruna; e qualli panni meglio se
acompagnano alle divise e alle nove livree d'imprese;
come significano, o amore, o speranza, o gelosia, e altre
simile cosse; come si deno portare le faldigie, come la
scufia in balzo riesse meglio, o coprendo tuti li capelli, o
lasiandone vedere un dito o dui; a qual donne reiscono
le orechie forate, come meglio se li confacino o le perle,
o le fila d'oro e in anella rivolte; le guise de' cassi come
vogliano essere a far parere il petto morbido e far mostrar
le mamelle, o poco o meno; gli monili, le catene d'oro,
le perle ordinate in filza come facino parere la donna piú
altera; de le anella ancora quali diti si debano ornare;
come deve movere il passo la donna, come deve ridere,
come vogliere li ochi, come far riverenza, e in quali atti
piú di grazia e piú di onestà si trova; come si dee fregiare
una vesta, e nove guise de agiongere diversi colori di
panni, che piú legiadri paiano.

E invero ho veduto in questa città molte madonne 20
tanto inordinatamente aconcie e ornate, che se a lor
stesse fussero cusí note come a chi le mira, se andariano
tute a riporre. Elle nel speglio con li proprii ochi si rimirano o al iudizio cieco delle fantesche si riportanto, le
quali piú presto de una scanceria di scutelle, che di ador-
namenti di donna saperiano iudicare. Alcune donne or-
dinano li capegli egualmente castigati e tuti ad un ordine
posti, che uno l'altro non passi; alcune, lassiandoli cossí
inordinati, hanno di acressimento di grazia e di beltà
tanto, che non si potria con mille lingue racontare.

Con soferenza vostra, madonna, tirate quella scufia un 21
dito piú inanci, che non si veggiano tanto e' capegli. Oh,
vedete che piú di grazia avete, perché il viso vostro è
alquanto scarno. Siché alla donna che mi riscoterà sarò
servo e fante, e uomo e femina. Piacendovi adunque uno

know everything about dressing a woman in outer garments, headgear, frills, plaits, and ruffs. I know which colors in fabrics are more flattering to the fair woman and which to the dark, which clothes go better with uniforms and the new liveries that have a coat of arms and a motto; what they signify: whether love, hope, jealousy, or other such things. I know how farthingales should be worn, whether a turban looks better covering all of one's hair or letting a little bit show; which women should have their ears pierced, whether they look better in pearls or in golden strands linked in rings. I know how to style bodices to contour the bosom and show a bit more or less of the breasts, how necklaces, golden chains, and strands of pearls may exalt a woman's style; then which fingers she should ornament with rings, how she should walk, laugh, avert her glance, bow, and in which gestures there is the most grace and propriety; how she should decorate a frock, and new ways of combining clothes of several colors to make them more attractive.

In this city, truly, I have seen ladies dressed and ornamented with such confusion that if they could see themselves through the eyes of people who look at them, they would all go and hide. Either they see themselves in the mirror with their own eyes or they rely on the blind judgment of their maids, who are more fit to judge a cupboardful of bowls than a lady's attire. Some women wear their hair so severe and orderly that no hair is out of place; others, by leaving their hair a bit disarranged, increase their grace and beauty more than a thousand tongues could say.

With your permission, madam, tug your cap a bit forward so that less hair shows. Oh, see how much more charm you have, because your face is rather narrow. Thus, to the woman who ransoms me I shall be servant and maid, man and woman. So if you like us, choose the

di noi, pigliarete quello che piú vi piace; che io non ho a dire altro, alli effeti remetendomi.

DORALICE. Bellissima, o bellissima virtú è questa altra! 22 E veramente io al iudizio della mia fante mi aconciai el capo questa matina, e vedete como stava fresca. Elle dicono poi, queste tristarelle, quando le si grida: «Voi sète fastidiosa, ella è bruta e vol che io la facia bella, mai non se li pò vivere...» Ma lassiamole con el malanno.

Invero, leggiadri giovени, le virtú vostre sonno soma- 23 mente da comendare e da esser tenute care da l'alteza de l'animo di qualunque donna. Io, per me, non posso comperar tante virtú, ma non potevate capitar in meglior cità di questa, perciò che ci sonno di gran signore e madonne, tanto amanti de le virtú, che creggio che con il sangue loro, non avendo altro modo, vi riscoteriano.

Cercate: sonno le donne di questa cità cortesi, generose, liberali, magnifiche. Io non son da porre nel numero loro, ché io son forestiera. Duolmi de la adversità vostra; ma cercate con bona speranza, che trovareti chi vi trarà de cossí fatto obrigo.

TANCREDI. Non poco ci adolciscono le vostre parole, 24 poiché vi dolete, gran mercè di Vostra Signoria. Siamo stati da alcune altre gentillissime madonne, da quali però grandissima speranza abiam riportato. Rimanetevi in pace.

DORALICE. Andate, che Idio ponga bon fine al vostro 25 desio. [Si ritira].

SCENA SECONDA

TANCREDI, GISMONDO e TEODORO

TANCREDI. Cortesi invero e piatose sonno le donne 26 di questa cità. Con quante dolci parole tutte hanno mostrato che 'l caso nostro gl'incresca. Gismondo, quella

one you like best. I have nothing else to say; I submit to the outcome.

DORALICE. Splendid, oh splendid is this last art! And to be sure I set my cap and hair this morning according to my maid's judgment, and you see how wrong she was. And then these wretched girls say when you scold them: "You are hard to please; she's ugly and she wants me to make her beautiful; they don't let you live. . . ." But leave them to their misfortune.

Truly, fair youths, your accomplishments are highly to be commended and cherished by any woman of high spirit. I myself cannot purchase such abilities, but you could not have come to a better city than this, where there are grandes dames and gentlewomen who so love these gentle arts that I think they would ransom you with their blood if it were the only way.

Look about; the women of this city are courteous, generous, liberal, magnificent. I am not one of their number as I am a visitor. Your adversity grieves me; but search with good hope and you will find someone to release you from your obligation.

TANCREDI. Your words comfort us not a little; for your commiseration, many thanks to your ladyship. We have been to see other noble ladies from whom we have taken great hope. Peace be with you.

DORALICE. Go, and may the Almighty bring your wish to a happy conclusion. [*She withdraws*].

SCENE TWO

TANCREDI, GISMONDO, and TEODORO

TANCREDI. In truth, the women of this city are courteous and compassionate. With how many sweet words have they all shown that they pity our plight. Gismondo,

61

con chi parlamo presente il marito, ti aveva sempre li
ochi adosso. Io mi creggio per certo che ella ti abbi a
riscotere.

GISMONDO. Volessello Idio.   27

TEODORO. Questo medesmo parve a me. Cerchiamo   28
altrove. Andiamo.

TANCREDI. Andiamo.

GISMONDO. Andiamo.

that one we spoke to while her husband stood by, she never took her eyes off you. I feel certain that she will pay your ransom.

GISMONDO. May it be the will of the Almighty.

TEODORO. I had the same impression. But let's look elsewhere. Let's go.

TANCREDI. Let's go.

GISMONDO. Let's go.

ATTO SECONDO

SCENA PRIMA

SIER TOMAO solo

SIER TOMAO. [*uscendo di casa*] El sè una gran cossa, che   1
son vegnúo in questa tera zà tre mesi, per muar àiere e
per star con l'anemo contento, che non me possa ancora
drezar a viver in pase con sta mia mogier. La vuol pur
che sempre buta via el mio, e contentar i suò apetiti, e
no varda a la mia impossibilitae.

La vuol adesso che traza un s-ciavo, che sè stao in man   2
de' Turchi, e tignirlo con essa per imparar vertue. E' la
vogio compiaser in questo, perché, se no 'l fesse, sempre
la me rosegherave, sempre la me tegnirave strucolao.
L'ha bona çiera de zovene; el sarà anche bon da altri ser-
vissii. La dise che 'l sa cossí ben cosir, cossí ben taiar, e
che l'ago ghe par tanto bon in man, e che 'l fica sempre
i ponti con tanta galantaria, con tanta misura... Che diavolo! La sè vertue anche questa galante e piasevole,
da done.

El sarà anche bon da vegnirme da drio anch'a mi per   3
fante, e sí credo che l'abia bona forza per vogar de mezo.
Che gran quantitae de dineri sè questa? E' 'nde spen-
derae volentiera el dopio, e poder aver el mio intento
con quela forestiera che son inamorao. Se mia mogier
averà sto s-ciavo, l'atenderà a l'ago, a farse taiar e stricar
le veste, e sí no me vardarà sempre drio, e sí no vorà
sempre saver donde son stao: «Che avèu fato da la tal? e
da la tal?» Anche mi sarò piú libero de quel che son.

Onde poràvio catar costori? Anche Ruzante ghe sè   4
andà drio anche esso, e sí no vien ni un ni l'altro. E' voio
andar çercando per le contrae. La vista no me serve tropo
ben: se no i vedo da lai, da lonzi no i porò figurar. Sto

ACT TWO

SCENE ONE

Sier Tomao alone

SIER TOMAO. [*leaving his house*] For a fact, I came to this territory three months ago for a change of air and some peace of mind and I still can't find a way to live peacefully with this wife of mine. She keeps wanting me to cast off my needs to satisfy hers, but she pays no attention to my limitations.

Now she wants me to ransom a slave who's been in the hands of the Turks; she wants him by her side so she can learn his virtues. I'm inclined to give in to her because if I don't she'll keep pestering me and clutching at my throat. He's a healthy-looking youth; he can perform other services too. She says he sews well and cuts and that the needle fits right in his hand, that he puts in the point with such civility, such rhythm . . . What the devil! Even that is a dashing and pleasing virtue—for women.

And he can come behind me as a serving boy, and yes I think he may be sturdy enough to come and go between us. Is it really so much money? I'd gladly spend twice as much to have my way with that foreign woman I crave. If my wife has this slave, she'll tend to his needle, having garments cut and fitted, and she won't be following me all the time, wanting to know where I've been: "What were you doing visiting this woman, or that?" I, too, will be freer than I am now.

Where can that fellow be? Ruzante went to look for him, and now neither one of them is here. I'll go and look in the streets. My eyesight doesn't serve me very well; if I don't see them up close, I won't be able to make them out from a distance. All this walking isn't good for

tanto caminar no fa a preposito per el mio cataro. E' me
voio voltar de qua, forsi i caterò. [*Esce*].

SCENA SECONDA

RUZANTE, poi BESSA

RUZANTE. [*solo, ansimante*] Cancaro a i Turchi e a i   5
Muori, e an a i pigè preson da' Turchi! A' he çercò bonamen tuta Pava, e sí a' n'i vezo. Orbéntena, chi n'ha
ventura, no vaga a pescare. La mia parona, che s'è andà
a inamorare in quel sberozaeto, in quel smenueto, che
par un luzo firto, e sí vuò che missiere ghe 'l scuoa, e sí
dise che la 'l vuò, perché el sa cossí ben taiare e cosire e
arpezare, e che 'l ghe piase tanto el so ovrar de gusela, e
che 'l sarà bon an per missiere. E elo ghe 'l vuò scuore,
e sí me ha mandò a çercare s'a' i cato.
    Cancaro el magne, l'è inamorà la mia parona in elo,   6
che a' 'l sè ben mi! Almanco favelésselo con a' fazón nu,
in malora, dasché la se ghe dêa inamorare! El va intoe-
scando con la lengua [*imita la pronuncia «moscheta» di Gismondo*], che l'amore che l'hano fato de la vita mia, che
lo sano fare de le scufie, che le pàrano bon... Cancaro el
magne! O cancaro, el m'è viso che a' i voiàn far biegi, i
punti; el m'è cossí doíso che la ['l] vuoia per altro ca per
cosire... A' me smaravegio lomé de sto vegio, che 'l [no]
se pense qualche male, che porà intravegnire. Ma sí, l'è
inamorò an elo, el se pensa d'altro. Orbéntena, l'amore
è orbo, el no ghe ve' gozo. A' sè che 'l ghe n'è tri de gi
amore su 'n pecolo: mata la scroa, mati i puorçiegi. El
me paron è inamorò in madona Rarize, e mi in la so
massarola, e la mia parona in quel turco pigiò da' Turchi.
Cancaro, l'è la bela noela!
    Se Diè m'ai', e' cherzo le indivinarla miegio mi ca ne-   7

my catarrh. I'll turn here; maybe I'll come across them.
[*He exits*].

SCENE TWO

RUZANTE, then BESSA

RUZANTE. [*alone, out of breath*] Blast the Turks and the
Moors and Turkish prisoners too! I've searched all over
Padua without seeing them. Very well, if you don't catch
fish, cut bait. My mistress has fallen for that piece of fluff,
that featherweight, who looks like a fried fish, and she
wants the master to ransom him; she wants him because
he can cut and sew and mend; she likes his needlework,
and he can serve the master too. So he's ready to ransom
him and has sent me to look for him.

Blast him, my mistress has fallen in love with him, I'm
sure of it! If he at least spoke the way we do, damn him,
since she had to fall in love! He goes around Tuscan-
twisting his tongue: [*he imitates Gismondo's Florentine
style*] "Thus has love made of my life that I make caps
she finds fair. . . ." Damn him. Oh blast it, in my opinion
they'll make some fine points, and for something besides
sewing . . . I'm only surprised that the old man doesn't
suspect some mischief. But he's in love himself and his
mind is elsewhere. Very well, love is blind, he doesn't see
a thing. But there are three loves growing on this stem:
mad the sow, mad the piglets. My master has fallen in
love with Lady Spicy, I'm in love with her maid, and my
mistress has fallen for that turkey captured by the Turks.
Damn, a fine new tale!

Lord help me, I understand it better than any of them.
I'll go see if I can find my girl and get her alone and talk
to her. I go all through the house, but I don't get a
chance to speak to her. [*He approaches Doralice's house, but*

gun d'egi. A' vuò andar a vêr s'a' la poesse mé vêre, e
catarla des–ciapà, e favelarghe. A' vago in casa da per
tuto, e sí a' n'he comilitè de favelarghe. [*Si avvicina alla
casa di Doralice, ma esita*] Pur che a' no me perda, con a'
la veza... Dègogi aspitare che la vegne, o che dègogi fare?
S'a' sbato a l'usso, so parona sentirà; s'a' no sbato, a' me
pora' fuossi cossí abirare, che la no vegnirae ancuò...

[*Origlia all'uscio*] Aldi, tasi?... A' sento pur sfreghezare.   8
A' vuò sigolare: [*fischia*] sbio, sbio... L'è miegio sbatere,
e muzare: [*bussa, e si allontana di corsa, saltellando*] ta, ta,
ta, don, don, don! [*Ripete*] A' vuò tornare: ta, ta, ta, don,
don, don! [*Si nasconde dietro un angolo e spia*].

BESSA. [*socchiudendo appena l'uscio*] Musi de giuti, as-   9
sèvo sechè le man! I sbate e po muza.

RUZANTE. [*fischia e si scopre*] Sbio, ohu! A' no vossè po   10
gnian ch'i l'aesse sechè... A' son stò mi. [*Le si avvicina*]
Con stèvo, an?

BESSA. Si' stò vu? A' crêa che 'l foesse stò sti musi de   11
giuti de tusi. A' sto ben, mi, e vu?

RUZANTE. A' starae ben, se no me fessè sgagnolire... A'   12
me fé pur stentare, mi.

BESSA. A' no fago stentar negun, mi. Che ve fàgogi?   13

RUZANTE. A' no me fé gniente, mo a' no me laghè   14
gnian far a mi.

BESSA. [*sarcastica*] A' si' ben de qui vergognusi che se   15
laga morire! N'aívu do man pichè al busto, da poerve
aiare?

RUZANTE. No, aldí, una cossa me conforta: che, con   16
dise quelú, vi', serore, una fià e' trognè, mo a' trognerè
an mi con questo [*gesto osceno*], e a corozar no vagia!

BESSA. A' no trogno de gnente. [*Con altro tono*] A' sè   17
che 'l no ve se pò pí sentire andar cantando da quenze.
Aí pur el bel soran,[1] se Diè m'ai'! Ch'a' son inamorò in
vu pí per el vostro ben cantare e bel balare, ch'a' no vîssi
mé, che 'l m'è viso che supia in Paraíso, co' a' v'aldo.

hesitates]. I just hope I don't lose my wits when I see her . . . Should I wait for her to come, or what shall I do? If I knock at the door, her mistress will hear; if I don't knock, I could lose my mind and she still won't come . . .

[*He puts his ear to the door*]. Listen, did you hear that? . . . I hear shuffling. I'll signal: [*he whistles*] whew, whew . . . It's better if I knock and then run: [*he knocks, and then he runs off, skipping*] ta, ta, ta, don, don, don! [*He repeats*]. I'll go back: ta, ta, ta, don, don, don! [*He hides around the corner and watches*].

BESSA. [*opening the door a crack*] Wicked mutts, I hope they wear their hands out! They knock and run.

RUZANTE. [*whistles and appears*] Whew, ho! I don't think you'd want them worn out . . . It was me. [*He approaches her*]. How are you doing?

BESSA. It was you? I thought it was those boys with the wicked mutts. I'm fine, and you?

RUZANTE. I'd be well if you didn't give me pangs . . . You really make me hurt.

BESSA. I don't hurt anyone. What have I done to you?

RUZANTE. You haven't done anything, but you don't let me do anything either.

BESSA. [*sarcastically*] Are you one of those helpless weaklings who let themselves die! Don't you have two arms attached to your sides so you can help yourself?

RUZANTE. Listen, one thing consoles me: this time, sister, you got me, as they say, but I'll get you back with this [*he makes an obscene gesture*] and it won't do any good to get angry.

BESSA. I don't want to get you. [*In a different tone*] I'm thinking that one doesn't hear any more singing in these parts. You sing a good top part, Lord help me! I fell in love with you for your singing and dancing; I'd never seen the like. I feel as if I'm in Paradise when I listen to you.

RUZANTE. [*schermendosi*] No, aldí, a' ve l'he dito, se- 18
rore, ancora, no me trognè.

BESSA. A la fe', a la fe', sora de l'anema mia, che a' no
ve trogno.

RUZANTE. Cancaro, mo se a' ne assè sentú l'altro diazo, 19
che a' ièrinu du, e sí a' cantavino in quatro, e mi a' fasea
de soran,[2] assè dito che a' sonàvino sogoluoti o pivi de
feraresi![3] A' se inorganàvino che le ose e 'l cantare andasea l'un in l'altro, che a' dissè: «I canta per ponto de
rason». Cancaro, el m'è viso che a' se [a]vignessan da mi
e vu, a cantare: mi a' farae de grosso e vu de sotile, o mi
de sora[n], con a' vossè, che a' la fassàn andare in lo àiere.

BESSA. A' se avignessan, se me vossè tanto ben, con a' 20
ve vuogio a vu.

RÚZANTE. Al sangue del cancaro, volzíve da qual lò a' 21
volí, a' ve buterae de soto da ben volere. Mo ve 'l poíssio
cossí mostrare con a' v' in vuogio, che, al sangue del
cancaro de merda, a' meno pí duramen la mia vita, pen-
sàntome de vu, che no fè mé can. El par che 'l me supia
stò becò el cuore da un gran bresparo, che 'l me se vaghe
sfregolanto per lo magon, per i buegi, tanto che 'l me
buta una insagna, una smagnia per adosso, che 'l par che
supia cargo de fuogo salbego. E po a' volí dir de ben
volere! A' ve vuò pí ben a vu, e sí a' so' pí inamorò in
vu, in lo fato vostro de vu, che no fo mé can de chiza.

BESSA. O Ruzante, i n'è tanti luvi in un s-ciapo! Se a' 22
me volí sí gran ben, ché no féo che 'l vostro paron, che
è inamorò in la mia parona, no guarde a dinari? Che a'
stassàn po tuti quatro de brigà, ché [a] altro muò no gh'è
ordene. Perché, aldí in la regia, l'è stò dito tanto male del
vostro paron a la mia parona... Puh sí! Che l'è de qua,
che l'è de là, e che... [*gli mormora sottovoce all'orecchio*].

RUZANTE. [*ascolta avido e annuisce*] A' intendo... Pota 23
del cancaro! A ela, de elo?... Sí, sí, sbossò, sí... Andè drio,
l'è vero... Poh! [*Ride*].

RUZANTE. [*defending himself*] Listen, I've told you once, sister, don't tease me.

BESSA. Faith, faith, on my soul, I'm not teasing you.

RUZANTE. Damn, if you had heard us the other day when there were two of us and we sang for four: I took the top part and you would have thought we were shawms or Ferrarese pipes, warbling 'til our voices and the singing flowed into one another. You'd have said: "They're singing for point of honor." Damn, I think you and I would sing well together; I'd take the bottom part and you the top, or I'd take the top part if that's what you want, and we'd reach up to heaven.

BESSA. We'd go well together if you love me as much as I love you.

RUZANTE. Blasted blood, take any part you want and I'll top you at love. If I could show you how much I want you, blasted bloody-shit, I live worse than a dog because of you. It's as if a big hornet had stung my heart and is buzzing in my stomach, through my guts, driving me mad, filling me with raging wild fire. And you talk about love! I love you more, I'm more in love with you, with everything about you, than ever a dog with his bitch.

BESSA. O Ruzante, these are too many wolves for one pack! If you love me so much why don't you see to it that your master, who's fallen for my mistress, pays no mind to the money? Then the four of us could keep company together; there's no other way; because, listen closely, people have told my mistress so many bad things about your master . . . Pooh, yes! That he has this here, and that there, and that. . . . [*she whispers in his ear*].

RUZANTE. [*listens attentively and nods*] I see . . . Blasted twat! To her, about him? Yes, yes, worn out, yes . . . Go on, it's true . . . Poh! [*He laughs*].

BESSA. [*concludendo*] A' stassàn po de brigà tuti.   24

RUZANTE. Mo me imprometívu fremamen? Mo to-
chème la man.

BESSA. [*gli porge la mano*] A' v'imprometo, e sí a' ve   25
atenderè.

RUZANTE. [*trattenendola tra le sue*] O man, maneta gu-   26
riosa... A' ve la vorae poér tuore senza far male, sta man,
a' ne avera' assé. L'è pur tofolota, a' si' pur tuta bela,
coluoría con è un pomo çielà.

BESSA. [*finge di commiserarsi, con civetteria*] Mé sí, a' me   27
hegi sentío d'agnora male, da no so che dí in qua. A'
vora' che a' me assè vezúa zà assé... Signore, a' iera pur
bela, a' iera pí sfripia che n'è na verza. Moa, a' vuò andare, che a' me sento ciamare. Volívuo vegnir su da madonna, vu? [*Si avvia alla porta per rientrare*].

RUZANTE. No, cancaro, a' tornerè ben. A' vuò andar a   28
ca', che 'l me paron me ha mandò a çercare no so che
preson de' Turchi, che 'l ne volea scuor un per mia madona. A' dirè che a' he çercò per tuto, e che a' n'i cato.
Moa, quel ch'è dito è dito; che no me fessè, po, inten-
dívu? Laghème pur far a mi de quelo, an, an? [*Fa un
cenno di saluto a Bessa, che rientra in casa e chiude*].

[*Solo*] Oh, cancaro me magne! A' m'he desmentegò el   29
meiore de dirghe, che a' ghe vuò ben. Mo a' ghe 'l dirè
un'altra fià. Cancaro, e' son pur venturin. L'è inamorò
in lo me balare e in lo me cantare, ela, a' ghe n'he inamorò de le altre, a la fe'. [*Muove qualche passo di danza*]
Tandaran, torirondon, torirondon! Laghème vêr s'a'
saesse far di qui pieripuoli, de qui revelin che i fa a
Pava... [*Eseguisce delle giravolte, sempre a passo di danza*]
Tirò, tirondò, tirondò! A' vuò andar mo a ca', che qui
Turchi de' esser tornè. I se arà acorto che la mia parona
ne averà vuogia de egi, i sarè tornè. Poh, mo con el vegio
sapia che quelú abia dito tanto mal de elo a madona
Rarize, el se despererà fremamen. Ossú, a' vuò andar a
ca'. [*Entra, spingendo l'uscio*].

BESSA. [*concluding*] We'll keep company together.

RUZANTE. Do you promise? Give me your hand.

BESSA. [*she gives him her hand*] It's a promise and I'll keep it.

RUZANTE. [*holding her hand in his*] O hand, pretty little hand . . . If I could take it without harming you, this hand would be enough for me; it's so supple, you're beautiful all over, colored like a ripe apple.

BESSA. [*pretending to feel sorry for herself, flirtatiously*] Well, yes, but I've been feeling poorly for some time now. I wish you had seen me a while ago. Lord, I really looked good, fresher than a cabbage. Oops, I have to go, she's calling me. Did you want to see my mistress? [*She approaches the door to go back in*].

RUZANTE. No, damn it, I'll come back. I have to go home because my master sent me to find some Turkish prisoners so he can ransom one for my lady. I'll say I looked everywhere without finding them. So, what's said is said; you won't disappoint me? You'll leave the rest to me then? [*He waves good-bye to Bessa, who goes back into the house and shuts the door*].

[*Alone*] Oh, canker eat me! I forgot to tell her the best part, that I love her. I'll tell her another time. Damn it, I'm lucky. She fell in love with my dancing and my singing, and faith, so have others. [*He dances a few steps*]. Tandaran, torirondon, torirondon! Let's see if I can do any turns, those pirouettes they do in Padua . . . [*He executes a turn, still dancing*]. Tiron, tirondon, tirondon! I'm going home; those Turkeys must have come back. They probably realized that my mistress wants them and came back. Poh, when the old man hears that someone has told Mistress Spicy so many bad things about him, he'll be desperate. Up now, I'm in. [*He goes in and closes the door*].

SCENA TERZA

Sier Tomao solo

SIER TOMAO. A le vagncli, e' me ho levao un gran   30
cargo da le spale, a rescuoder sto s-ciavo a mia moier.
L'atenderà mo a farse taiar a esso nuove sise, de cassi, de
invistiure, e de sto diavolo de sbalçi, che, co' i sè pí grossi
e pí grandi, i ghe piase pí e sí dise che le par meio.

E' poderò mo atender al mio amor, intravignando
l'inzegno de Ruzante de mezo, che me dreza su la via
che abia mio intento. Benché credo che sarà gran fadiga,
ché sto bestion sè tanto pregro che mai no compie. El sè
do ore che 'l sè andao a çercar sti s-ciavi, e sí no vien
mai, gnanche no se pensa che i poderave esser tornai a
casa... L'ha pí de l'aseno ca del cavalo!

[*Inforca gli occhiali*] E' me voio meter i ociali, se 'l ve-   31
desse mai. [*Si guarda intorno*] E' no 'l vedo. E' voio andar
spassizando davanti casa de madona Doralice... In sto
mezo el porave vegnir. [*Muove qualche passo*].

SCENA QUARTA

Ruzante e Sier Tomao

RUZANTE. [*uscendo di casa*] Po po po pota del cancaro!   32
Che hegio aldío, che hegio sentío, che hegio vezú mé a
sto mondo? Rescuore un omo, e essere una femena. Al
sangue del cancaro, l'ha crezú rescuoere un mas-cio, e sí
ha rescovú una mas-cia. L'ha fato con fè Dondo, che
crête comprar una spa', e sí comprò lomé la guaina; e co'
'l vuosse meter la man sul màneg o, el catè lomé la busa
de la guaina... [*Ride*] Pota, mo l'è la gran noela, questa.
Chi n'ara' mo crezú che colú fusse sto un omo? La mia

SCENE THREE

SIER TOMAO alone

SIER TOMAO. By the gospel, I've lifted a great weight from my shoulders by ransoming that slave for my wife. Now she'll keep busy having him cut new styles of frocks, corselets, cloaks, and those devilish turbans: the thicker and bigger they are, the more they like them and the better they think they look.

And I can put my mind to my own love affair, with Ruzante's wit plying in between, steering me toward my goal. But it will take plenty of effort because there's no end to that dolt's laziness. It's been two hours since he went looking for those slaves and he's still not back; he doesn't even realize that they may have returned home . . . He's more ass than horse!

[*He puts on his glasses*]. Maybe if I put on my spectacles I'll see him. [*He looks around*]. He's not in sight. Very well, I'll take a stroll in front of Madam Doralice's house . . . Meanwhile he may come. [*He takes a few steps*].

SCENE FOUR

RUZANTE and SIER TOMAO

RUZANTE. [*coming out of the house*] Po po po pox of a piece! What have I heard, what have I felt, whatever in this world have I seen? Ransom a man and get a woman. Blasted blood, he thought he was paying ransom for a male and instead he ransomed a female. He's like Dondo, who thought he was buying a sword but only bought the sheath, then when he reached for the handle he just felt an empty space . . . [*He laughs*]. Twat, this is a good story. Who would have thought that creature

parona pianze, la se sbate, la se tribola, che 'l par che 'l
ghe supia morto pare e mare. Oh, ch'a' no cusirón pí,
ché la gusela ha scavazò la ponta! A' no taierón pí gonele
a la devisa, a' no farón pí strapunti né sorapunti, ché le
forbese è deventè smozegon! El me ven quel cancaro da
riso, ch'a' cago da per tuto, ah, ah, ah!...

SIER TOMAO. Chi diavolo è costú che vien ridando? L'è   33
esso. [*Lo investe*] On' diavolo èstu stao imbusao? Ti me
fa parer una bestia insensao, a çercarte tuto ancúo.

RUZANTE. Mo a' iera andò çercanto qui che me man-   34
diessi, e sí a' no gi he catè mé. A' he çercò bonamen per
tuta Pava. A' son po stò là, saíu?

SIER TOMAO. Onde là?

RUZANTE. Da madona Rarize.

SIER TOMAO. Co' madona Rarize? Madona Doraliçe,
ti vuol dir.

RUZANTE. Missier sí, missier sí, a' son stò là.

SIER TOMAO. Ben, co' hastu fato, fio belo?   35

RUZANTE. Mo aéa paura de star massa, e de fato a' diè   36
spazamento, e sí a' torniè a ca'.

SIER TOMAO. Ben, hastu visto el preson che ho rescosso? Piàselo a madona?

RUZANTE. Cancar'è che a' l'he vezú! A' sassè cativo da   37
comprar bestiame, vu, tossè una mas-cia per un mas-cio,
una porçela per un vereto.

SIER TOMAO. Co', cossí?

RUZANTE. Mo l'è una femena, quelú che aí rescoú, e   38
madona l'ha vezú e tocò.

SIER TOMAO. Co' diavolo una femena? Che dirastu?

RUZANTE. Mo a' sè ch'al pissare l'è una femena, mi; e   39
madona pianze, e sí se trúbula, che la no averà mé ben,
che la è pí desgrazià de le altre, che la se aéa pensò de far
fare e de dire, e che la se ha catò le man pine de brusche.
Una pianze, l'altra sgnica, che aéa tanto riso che cagava

wasn't a man? My mistress is weeping, writhing, despairing, as if her father and mother had died. Oh, we'll sew no more, for the needle's point has broken! We'll cut no more skirts split down the middle, we'll have no more needlepoints, or pricks, because the scissors have gone blunt! I laughed so blasted hard I pooped, ha, ha, ha! . . .

SIER TOMAO. Who the devil is that coming along laughing? It's him. [*He starts in*]. Where the devil have you been hiding? You make me look like a dumb animal, looking for you all day.

RUZANTE. I went looking for those people you sent me after, but I couldn't find them. I looked all over Padua. Then I went over there, you know where I mean?

SIER TOMAO. Where is "there"?

RUZANTE. Mistress Spicy's house.

SIER TOMAO. Mistress Spicy? You mean Lady Doralice.

RUZANTE. Yes master, yes master, there's where I've been.

SIER TOMAO. Very well, dear boy, how did it go?

RUZANTE. I was afraid to stay too long so I left quickly and returned home.

SIER TOMAO. Well, did you see the prisoner whose ransom I paid? Does the mistress like him?

RUZANTE. Damn, did I see him! You'd make a rotten livestock buyer, you would, mistaking a sow for a swine, a gilt for a boar.

SIER TOMAO. What's this?

RUZANTE. She's female, the person you ransomed, and milady saw and touched.

SIER TOMAO. How in the devil female? What are you saying?

RUZANTE. By the way she pisses, to me, she's female; and milady is crying and despairing that she'll never be happy, that she's worse off than other women, that she'd thought he'd do this and say that, and now she finds her hands full of splinters. One weeps, the other wails; I

da per tuto... A' me son tolto via, e sí a' l'he laghè sgnicare.

SIER TOMAO. Che besogna che mia moier se destruza 40 né che la pianza? El sè meio per essa che la sia una femina, la ghe farà compagnia. E' 'nde son anche mi pí contento, ché avea qualche sospizion. [*Rimuginando*] Una femena, l'è cara per quei danari.

RUZANTE. La no fa tanto per ela, quanto per l'ato, ch'è 41 stò burto. E po el ghe recresse pí de vu, perché el sara' stò bon da vegnirve drio a vu, e per questo madona se trúbola.

SIER TOMAO. No seràstu cossí bon ti, che ti ha çiera de 42 esser pí gaiardo? Ché elo aveva una çiera de smenueto, da poca forza... Ti [ti] sè ben informao d'i tuò membri. [*Lo valuta con un'occhiata*].

RUZANTE. [*ammiccando*] L'è vera, mo mi no porè fuossi 43 atendere a desgramegnar tante vanieze... Ché 'l besogna che vaghe in qua e in là, intendíu?

SIER TOMAO. [*seccato, con un'alzata di spalle*] A so posta, 44 mal viazo essa! [*Con altro tono, ansioso*] Dime un puoco, co' ti ha fato là, ben? Hastu parlao con essa? L'hastu vista? Hastu parlao con essa?

RUZANTE. Missier no, a' he favelò con la so massarola. 45 Puh sí, s'a' saessè... [*Scuote il capo*].

SIER TOMAO. Che, caro fio belo? Di' via.

RUZANTE. Mo no èla inamorò in mi, la puta? Che la 46 frègola el cul da per tuto, e che la è inamorà in lo me cantare, puh sí, e che no gh'è stò mé negun che l'abia possú far inamorare, lomé mi, puh sí, e che a' he gi uoci che, con a' vuogio, a' le fazo inamorar le pute, puh sí...

SIER TOMAO. Oh, te vegna el cancaro! Ti ha bon, 47 donca? Onde te hala aldío cantar? Che canzon cantàvestu: stramboti o barzelete?[1]

RUZANTE. Stramuoti,[2] missier no. La me ha aldío de 48 fuora, ch'a' cantàvino me e un altro d'i Sgnanferlati[3]...

laughed so hard I pooped in my pants . . . I tore myself away and I left them wailing.

SIER TOMAO. Why must my wife despair, or weep? A female is better for her; she'll keep her company. I'm happier too, because I had certain suspicions. [*Brooding*] That's a lot to pay though, for a female.

RUZANTE. It's not for herself so much as for the transaction that went sour. And then she's sorry on your account, because a man would have been sturdy enough to follow behind you as well; that's what milady regrets.

SIER TOMAO. Couldn't you do that? You have a hardier look. That other one looked skinny and puny. Your parts are well formed. [*He sizes him up with a glance*].

RUZANTE. [*winking*] That's true, but I may not be able to cultivate so many furrows . . . where it's necessary to go this way and that, you know what I mean?

SIER TOMAO. [*fed up, with a shrug*] It's her affair, worse for her! [*In a different tone, anxiously*] Tell me, how did it go there? Have you spoken to her? Did you see her? Did you speak to her?

RUZANTE. No master, I spoke with her maid. Oh yes, if you knew . . . [*He shakes his head*].

SIER TOMAO. What, dear boy? Go on.

RUZANTE. Well, isn't that girl in love with me? She shakes her ass in every direction, and says she fell in love with my singing, oh, yes, and that no one else ever made her fall in love, only me, oh, yes! and that with my eyes I can make girls fall in love, oh yes . . .

SIER TOMAO. Oh, canker consume you! She likes you, does she? Where did she hear you sing? What kind of songs were you singing: merry or serious?

RUZANTE. Delirious? No, sir. She heard me when I was singing outside, another Mr. Blocknose and I . . .

Che la dise ch'a' he el pí bel soran che la vêsse mé, e 'l pí
gaiardo, che sempre mé sta in l'àire, puh sí.

SIER TOMAO. Che canzon cantàvestu? Canzon che se 49
usa adesso, o pur canzon vecie?

RUZANTE. Cantava de «La mala morte»,[4] de «Dal mio 50
amore, ch'a' mi son stato»... puh sí, de «Levami de una
bela matina», che sège mi, mo a' cantava mi solo... de
«Stela Diana, stela relusente», de «che fa' spiendore mo a
tuta questa zente»... Va' là, po a' fasea perché el no paresse che cantasse per ela, e ela de fato sboría fuora. [Ac-
cenna, via via che le ricorda, all'aria delle canzoni].

SIER TOMAO. Ti ha una bona bose, e una bona sgorza. 51
O se ti savessi le canzon che so mi, o che mi avesse la
bose che ti ha ti, cantéssemo ben. Se te bastasse l'anemo de impararne qualche una, te 'nde darave quatro o
çinque.

RUZANTE. Dîle pur, messiere, mo di' de le pí bele.

SIER TOMAO. [attacca, con tono ispirato] 52

«El papa sí ha concesso quindese ani»...[5]

RUZANTE. Ma sí, papa! La merda, papa! Dîme canzon 53
che dighe de lo amore, che «lo me hano fato de la
vita mia»...

SIER TOMAO. Aldi quest'altra; ti no ha inteligenzia, 54
però le te despiase.

«Andemo, amanti, tuti in Barbaria»...[6]

RUZANTE. Che, a farse rasare, in la barbaria? El ghe 55
vuol altro ca esser rasè, a la fe', a piasere a le pute. El
besogna che le abia don' pigiare, e no esser rasè. La n'è
bela gnan questa, la no menzona de lo amore. Disène
una cossí: «Anema mia, se sola te catasse», o «Cavato ve
voria esser lo core», o «Cortelo in lo magon per mezo el
core»... De queste, che menzone core, amore de la vita
mia, ché altramen le n'è bele.

SIER TOMAO. Aldi. [Canta]

She says I have the best top voice she's ever heard, the strongest, and that it always holds up high, oh, yes.

SIER TOMAO. What songs were you singing? Songs they sing today or an old song?

RUZANTE. I was singing "Sad Death" and "I Have Been to See My Love" . . . and, oh yes, "I Awoke One Fair Morning," I remember I was singing alone: "Star Diana, shining star, you shed light upon everyone." Well, I pretended not to be singing for her and she came right outside. [*Little by little he remembers the tunes*].

SIER TOMAO. You have a good voice and a good throat. Oh, if you knew the songs that I know, or if I had your voice, we would sing well together. If you have a mind to learn any, I could teach you four or five.

RUZANTE. Go right ahead, master, but teach me the best ones.

SIER TOMAO. [*begins confidently*]

> The pope has granted fifteen years. . . .

RUZANTE. Pope indeed! Pope, poop! Teach me songs about love. "They have made my life. . . ."

SIER TOMAO. Listen to this one; you don't understand them, that's why you don't like them.

> Let us go, lovers all, to Barbaria. . . .

RUZANTE. To the barber's? for a shave? It takes more than a shave, by my faith, to satisfy girls. They want something they can hold on to, that's not shaved. That one's no good either; it doesn't mention love. Teach me one that goes like this: "My soul, if I caught you alone," or "I'd like to see your heart torn from you," or "Knife in the chest right through the heart" . . . songs like these that mention the heart, the love of my life; otherwise they're useless.

SIER TOMAO. Listen. [*He sings*]

«Quatro sospiri te voria mandare[7]   56
e mi meschino fosse ambassatore»...

Te piase questa, mo?

RUZANTE. Missier sí. Oh, de sti sospiri... A' vora' mo   57
che la diesse de mi, e no de vu.

SIER TOMAO. Aldi, bestia, ti no intendi. La canzon dise   58
cossí; ti la puol voltar può, perché, quando ti canti ti, el
par che ti sii ti. [Canta]

«Quatro sospiri te voria mandare
e mi meschino fosse ambassatore»...

RUZANTE. [di nuovo interrompendolo] Mo vi' mo che la   59
dise de vu: «e mi meschino»... Sbio, cope, Fiorin! «e mi
meschino». A' me la vossè cazare in lo carniero, vu,
compagnon! Con a' la cantasse, a' la canterae per vu.

SIER TOMAO. No, diavolo! Lassa che compia, se te   60
piase.

RUZANTE. A' vora' che avessè bel' e compío, mi. Di'   61
pur, che a' ve ascolterè.

SIER TOMAO. [canta]

«Quatro sospiri te voria mandare   62
e mi meschino fosse ambassatore:
lo primo sí te deza salutare,
l'altro te conte lo mio gran dolore;
lo terzo sí te deza assai pregare,
che tu confermi questo nostro amore;
e lo quarto te mando inamorato,
no me lassar morir desconsolato».

RUZANTE. Vi', mo a' la sè an mi, questa. Mo la no va a   63
sto muò, la dise:

«La mia cara serore, bela de Biranza,
no me lassar morir desconsolato.
Dorindon, dorindon, dorindon»...

[Muove qualche passo di danza].

> Four sighs would I send
> And my wretched self convey . . .

You like this one, don't you?

RUZANTE. Yes, sir. Oh, those sighs . . . But I want it to be about me; not you.

SIER TOMAO. Listen, dolt, you don't understand. The song goes like that; you can turn it around because when you sing it, it's as if it were about you. [*He sings*].

> Four sighs would I send
> And my wretched self convey . . .

RUZANTE. [*interrupting him again*] Don't you see that it's about you: "my wretched self . . ." I'll bet on it! "My wretched self." You're pulling my leg, pal. If I sang it, I'd be singing about you.

SIER TOMAO. Go to the devil! Let me finish, will you please.

RUZANTE. I wish you were finished for good. But go on; I'm listening.

SIER TOMAO. [*He sings*].

> Four sighs would I send,
> And my wretched self convey;
> Let the first a greeting tend,
> The next my grief relay;
> The third begs you to bend
> And let our love hold sway.
> The fourth I send thee lovingly,
> Lest disconsolate death be my destiny.

RUZANTE. Yes, I know that one too; but this is how it goes:

> Dear girl, beauty of Biranza
> Don't let me die without an answer.
> Dorindon, dorindon, dorindon . . .

[*He dances a few steps*].

SIER TOMAO. [*lo osserva divertito*] Eh, eh, ti me fa pur 64
rider! Ti diè aver nome Ruzante perché ti ruzi sempre,
n'è vero?

RUZANTE. El me derto lome è Perduòçimo. Mo 65
quando iera putato, che andasea con le biestie, sempre
mé a' ruzava o con cavale, o con vache, o con scroe, o
con piegore. E po aéa un can, che a' me aéa arlevò, che
a' l'aéa usò ch'a' me 'l menava a man, ch'a' dissè: «L'è un
asenelo». A' ruzava sempre mé con elo, a' ghe spuava in
lo volto, pur che a' me poesse des-ciapar e andar drio
qualche macion a ruzar con elo. E perzòntena i me messe
lome Ruzante, perché a' ruzava.

SIER TOMAO. La ghe va! [*Con altro tono*] Ben, che dise 66
madona Doraliçe? Hastu parlao con essa?

RUZANTE. Mi a' cherzo ch'a' no farí gnente, per 67
quanto me ha dito la so massarola (ché co ela a' n'he
favelò), perché el gh'è stò dito tante zanze, tante noele,
che l'è el cancaro.

SIER TOMAO. [*allarmato*] Co' zanze? Co' novele? Chi 68
ghe ha dito ste zanze? Chi sè stao?

RUZANTE. A' no sè chi 'l supia stò. El ghe ha dito, a 69
ela: «Ti è inamorà in quel vecio, in quel vecio sbossò?»
E che a' si' scarso co' è na pétema, e che se a' la veessè
morire, a' no spendessè un beço, e co' arí abú zò che a'
vorí, che a' no ve drezassè dal scagno per farghe un servissio, e che 'l ve puza el fiò a muò de vovi marzi, e che
i piè e i scagi ve puza de freschinazo, da ongie de cavalo
morto, che 'l no se ve pò star a pè.

SIER TOMAO. Mi, mi? O diavolo, can, laro, mi, an? 70
[*Freme*].

RUZANTE. Vu, missier sí. Aldí, e che se ghe stassè a pè 71
una note, la imboasse[ssè] tuta, che 'l parae che 'l ghe
foesse andò lumeghe per adosso; e che a' fé tal sgargaion,
che par un gran schiton de cioca, e che a' ghe fé drio tal
corezon, che 'l sona un s-ciopeto, e che aí tanta chila,

SIER TOMAO. [*observes him with amusement*] Eh, eh, you make me laugh! Your name must be Ruzante because you always play rough, is that so?

RUZANTE. My real name is Perduoçimo. But when I was a boy and tended animals, I always roughed it up with horses or cows or sows or sheep. Then I had a dog, one I had raised and trained to follow along by my hand; you would have said, "He's a little ass." I always played a ruse on him: I'd spit in his face so I could slip behind some bush to play rough. That's why they call me Ruzante, because I play a rough ruse.

SIER TOMAO. It suits you! [*Changing his tone of voice*] Well, what does mistress Doralice say? Have you spoken to her?

RUZANTE. I don't think you'll get anywhere with her after what her maid told me (she's the one I spoke to), because someone told her mistress so much gossip, so many stories, it's a disaster.

SIER TOMAO. [*alarmed*] Gossip? Stories? Who has spread this gossip? Who?

RUZANTE. I don't know who it was; he said: "Have you fallen for that old man, that worn-out old man?" That you're as stingy as a godwit, that if she were dying you wouldn't spend a lira, that once you've had what you want you won't budge an inch to do anything for her; and that your breath stinks like rotten eggs, and your feet and armpits smell musty, like the hooves of a dead horse, so no one can stand to be close to you.

SIER TOMAO. I? I? O devil, dog, thief, I? [*He trembles*].

RUZANTE. Yes, master, you. And listen to this: that if she were to spend the night with you she'd get as filthy as if snails had passed over her, that you cough like a cackling hen, that your farts sound like gunshots, that

che 'l par un cassil da piva, e che per questo a' no poí caminar inviò.

SIER TOMAO. [*esterrefatto*] O diavolo, o diavolo, varda   72
zò che i se ha impensao de dir. Se no fosse qua, e' te farave pur veder, e sí ti tocheravi con man, che 'l mente per la gola, sto laro. Chi diavolo è costú?

RUZANTE. A' cherzo che 'l supie stò un scolaro. [*Come*   73
ricordandosene allora, aggiunge] Puh, aldí, e che aí no so che altro mal, in le neghe.

SIER TOMAO. Che mi me vaga a negar?   74

RUZANTE. Vu, missier, che aí no so che mal in le   75
neghe, de drio del sgureguzo...

SIER TOMAO. In le nadeghe, ti vol dir?

RUZANTE. Missier sí, missier sí. Un male a muò sbar-   76
dele, smarsarele, merdarele, a' no sè ben dire...

SIER TOMAO. Maroele, ti vol dir?

RUZANTE. Missier sí, missier sí, che 'l par ch'a' fazè un   77
puto, quando a' caghè.

SIER TOMAO. El mente per la gola. No 'l saveràvestu ti?   78
Ti me ha pur visto cagar.

RUZANTE. [*continua imperterrito*] Puh sí, e che a' si'   79
sbossò, e che a' parí fato co un cortelazo, e che despoiò in zuparelo a' parí un Rigobelo[8] e na spauraia da co-lombi, e aí una spala pí elta de l'altra un gran pè, e che parí un galo sberozò... Puh sí, a' no ve pora' mé rivar de dire.

SIER TOMAO. Che diavolo no respondèstu che 'l no   80
iera vero?

RUZANTE. A' disea che no ve he mé vezú in zuparelo   81
despoiò, e che 'l porae essere, mo tamentre che a' no 'l crêa.

SIER TOMAO. E' voio pur che ti vedi. Zafa qua sta ma-   82
nega, tira. [*Ruzante lo aiuta a liberarsi della sopravveste*]. Te pario mo sí desfigurao?

RUZANTE. [*ammirandolo*] A' si' derto co' è un scato, vu!   83

you have a hernia like bagpipes and that's why you can't walk fast.

SIER TOMAO. [*aghast*] Oh the devil, the devil, look what he's invented. If we were not out here I'd let you see for yourself; you could feel with your own hand that he lies in his throat, this thief. Who the devil is he?

RUZANTE. I think it was some scholar. [*As if remembering, he adds*] And listen to this: he told her something else is wrong, with your bottom.

SIER TOMAO. He'll send me to the bottom?

RUZANTE. That you, master, have something wrong with your bottom, your butt . . .

SIER TOMAO. My buttocks?

RUZANTE. Yes, master; yes, master . . . some problem like saddles, shingles, merds, I don't know the exact name . . .

SIER TOMAO. Do you mean hemorrhoids?

RUZANTE. Yes, master, yes; that it's as if you were having a baby when you shit.

SIER TOMAO. He lies in his throat. You know that, don't you? You've seen me shit.

RUZANTE. [*he continues unperturbed*] Yes, and that you're worn out and look as if you were carved with a dull blade, and that undressed to your doublet you look like a clown and a scarecrow; that one of your shoulders is a good foot higher than the other, and you look like a castrated cock . . . Pooh, I could go on.

SIER TOMAO. Why the devil didn't you answer that it's not true?

RUZANTE. I said I had never seen you stripped to your doublet, and it might be so, but that I, nevertheless, did not believe it.

SIER TOMAO. I want you to have a look. Grab this sleeve and pull. [*Ruzante helps him remove his jacket*]. Am I so disfigured?

RUZANTE. [*admiring him*] You're straight as an arrow,

Caminè mo pian, volzíve mo da l'altro lò... no, da st'altro... da l'altro... Oh, trotè mo inviò.

SIER TOMAO. Co' trotar? Che tombola, ti vol dir? 84

RUZANTE. Missier sí, ché a' ieri stombolò, vu. Caminè 85
de troton, cossí, vi'... [*Fa qualche passo di corsa*] Oh, ca-
zève mo a corere.

SIER TOMAO. [*corre attorno alla scena, trascinando le gambe;* 86
quindi incespica e cade lungo disteso] Iesu, songio vasto? Me
hoio fato gran mal?

RUZANTE. [*aiutandolo a rialzarsi*] Missier no, a' no 'í 87
mal negun. Poh, a comuò a' si' cossí incapò?

SIER TOMAO. El sè stao sti zocoli, che mal viazo essi! 88

RUZANTE. Al sangue del cancaro, che i mente per la 89
gola, che si' gaiardo, idente su le gambe, con è un bel
levriero. Cancaro i magne! L'è lomé che i dise che a' si'
tanto scarso; e le femene tra' a i dinari, perché a' saí pur
che con i dinari se fa zò che se vuò. El besogna che a' no
supiè sí scarso.

SIER TOMAO. Torna là adesso, e di' che, se l'ha bisogno 90
de danari, che la me comanda; e che la no voia vardar a
zanze de sti lari, che per invidia dise ste parole. E che la
puol esser çerta che mi no andarò ancúo drio a questa,
doman drio a quel'altra, co' fa i zoveni, che quela che
ghe fa pí apiaseri, essi ghe vol manco ben. E che veste e
danari no ghe mancherà, e che la serà dona e madona del
mio, che la 'l manizerà come ghe piaserà, pur che la me
voia ben. Va' via, fio belo, adesso adesso, che mi andarò
a casa a veder zò che fa madona. Va' via, e torna presto.

RUZANTE. A' andarè ontiera, e sí a' ghe dirè—laghè 91
pur far a mi—che a' v'he vezú, e che a' si' derto co' è
na ferza in la schina, e che aí na gamba trelada—laghè
pur far a mi—, e che a' ghe volí ben a ela; e che no aí
mé ben, se ela no ve vo' ben, perché vu de ela, o vussi
dir ela de vu, che na fià la no guarde a dinari—laghè pur
far a mi.

you are! Walk slowly; now turn the other way . . . no, this way . . . that way . . . Oh, try to jog.

SIER TOMAO. What do you mean, jog? Trot, is that what you mean?

RUZANTE. Yes, master, because yesterday you tottered. Walk fast, like this. Watch [*He takes a few quick steps*]. Now break into a run.

SIER TOMAO. [*he runs around, dragging his legs; then he stumbles and falls flat*] Jesus, am I injured? Did I hurt myself badly?

RUZANTE. [*helping him to get up*] No, master, you're not hurt at all. Poh, how did you trip like that?

SIER TOMAO. It was these wooden clogs, damn them!

RUZANTE. Blasted blood, they lie in their throats; you're vigorous, and as steady on your legs as a fine greyhound. Damn them to hell! The worst is that they say you're stingy; and women care about money, because as you well know, with money you can do what you want. You mustn't be so stingy.

SIER TOMAO. Go back there now and say that if she needs any money, she should ask me; and tell her not to pay attention to these gossiping thieves, who say these things out of envy. And tell her she can be certain that I won't be chasing one girl today and another tomorrow, like young men, who love a girl less the more she tries to please them. And that she'll not want for clothes or money, and she will be my lady and mistress of what is mine, to manage as she likes, so long as she loves me. Go on, dear boy, right now, while I go home to see what madame is doing. Go on and come back quickly.

RUZANTE. I'll go gladly, and I'll say—leave it to me— that I've seen you, and your back is straight as an arrow, that you have a shapely leg—leave it to me—and that you love her; and that you'll never be content unless she loves you, because between you and her, or between her and you, money is no object—leave it to me.

SIER TOMAO. Aldi, torna presto, mo no me dir che ma-   92
dona alda, sastu?

RUZANTE. A' ghe 'l dirè, che la me alda lomé da ela e   93
da mi.

SIER TOMAO. Aldi, dighe che ti me ha visto despoiao,   94
e che ho bela persona. Mo no dir che sia cazúo per
gnente.

RUZANTE. No, missier no, cancaro! A' son pí scaltrío   95
ch'a' no cri'. [*Si avvia*].

SIER TOMAO. Aldi, aldi... [*Lo richiama, come per aggiun-*   96
gere qualcosa, poi non ne fa nulla] Va' via, no te voio dir
altro. Fa' pí presto che ti pol. [*Parte*].

RUZANTE. Laghème pur far a mi. [*Solo*] Cancaro, l'è   97
stà la bela noela. A' l'he mo fato despoiare, el dè un sta-
leson in tera, che 'l sonè un gran çefon che caísse. L'in-
traven pur le gran noele, e chi la diesse, questa, el no gh'è
cuore che 'l crêsse: un vecio, che ha otanta agni pichè al
culo, supia inamorò... [*Si appressa alla porta di Doralice*]
A' cherzo che l'usso è averto. Olà, olà, o da la ca'? A'
vegnirè de longo, mi. Gh'è can? [*Entra*].

SIER TOMAO. Listen, come back quickly, but don't say anything to me that madame can hear, do you understand?

RUZANTE. I'll tell it in such a way that she thinks it is between her and me.

SIER TOMAO. Listen, tell her you've seen me undressed and I cut a fine figure. But don't say that I tripped on any account.

RUZANTE. No, master, no, damn it. I'm more cunning than you think. [*He withdraws*].

SIER TOMAO. Listen, listen . . . [*He calls him back as if to add something, then says nothing*]. Go ahead, I have nothing else to say. Do it as quickly as you can. [*He leaves*].

RUZANTE. Leave it to me. [*Alone*] Damn, that was a good plot. I got him to undress and he fell to the ground, toppled like the trunk of a tree. Strange things happen, and if someone were to tell this story not a soul would believe it; an old man with eighty years on his back in love . . . [*He approaches Doralice's door*]. I think the door is open. Ola, ola, is anyone home? I'll go right in. Is there a dog here? [*He enters*].

GINEVRA. Guarda che né per piaza né a l'ostaria ti   1
uscisse di boca che io fusse femina, per quanto hai cara
la salute mia; ma dimi in nome de uomo ogni cossa.

GHITTA. Madonna sí, non vi dubitate, che sarò ben
acorta.

GINEVRA. A ora te lo dissi, dimi: «Missier sí», e chia-   2
mami patron, e dimi per nome messer Caco.

GHITTA. Come voleti che vi chiama? Caca?   3

GINEVRA. Caco, Caco, smemorata.

GHITTA. Caco, madonna? Oh, è troppo bruto nome, è   4
piú neto nome Pisso, che Cacco.

GINEVRA. Taci, per la tua fe', né un né l'altro non mi   5
dire. Tu hai cossí poco cervelo, che, due parole o tre che
dicesti, saria scoperta e in eterno vituperata.

GHITTA. [*accennando all'abito maschile della padrona*] Vi-   6
tuperata potrai esser piú presto in questo abito, perché,
per quanto si dice, el Studio[1] è in questa terra, e dotori
e scolari, che sono gioveni, piú presto li gioveni che le
donne rimirano, e, se ti vegono, ti verano drieto, credendo che tu sie un scolaro, per cognoserti o per prati-
carti. Il che non verria, se in abito di donna fusti vestita,
ché crederiano che fusti una matrona di questa città.

GINEVRA. Taci, bestia, ché in questo abito potremo gir   7
piú sicuramente. Al primo, che allo incontro ci vegna,
voglio dimandar di loro; facilmente intenderemo, ma
voglio fingere ch'io cerchi de un mio fratello, e non de
uno amante. E tu guarda di stare in cervello, se sarai adi-
mandata a rispondere.

ACT THREE

SCENE ONE

GINEVRA and GHITTA

GINEVRA. Be careful not to let it from your lips either in the piazza or at the inn that I am female, if you care about my well-being; address me in every matter as if I were a man.

GHITTA. Yes, milady, doubt it not. I'll be very careful.

GINEVRA. I just told you to answer me: "yes, milord"; call me master and address me by the name of Master Caco.

GHITTA. You want me to call you Caca?

GINEVRA. Caco, Caco, silly girl.

GHITTA. Caco, milady? Oh, that's too ugly. Pisso is a nicer name than Cacaco.

GINEVRA. Quiet, by your faith, don't call me either one. You have so little sense that two or three words from you and I would be found out and disgraced forever.

GHITTA. [*pointing to her mistress's male clothing*] You'd sooner be disgraced in this outfit because the University is in this city, and they say that professors and scholars, the young ones, have an eye for young men rather than women, and if they approach you to make your acquaintance it will be from the rear if they think you're a student. That wouldn't happen if you were dressed like a woman; then they would think you were a matron of this city.

GINEVRA. Silence, senseless creature; in these clothes we'll be able to move about more safely. I'll inquire about them from the first person we meet; we'll be easily informed, but I want to pretend that I'm looking for a brother of mine, not a lover. And you keep your wits about you if you are asked to respond.

Oh, colui che esce di quella casa, sarà forse buono per informarci. [*A Ruzante, che esce in quel mentre dalla casa di Doralice*] Ascolta, tu.

SCENA SECONDA

RUZANTE, GINEVRA e GHITTA

RUZANTE. [*sulla porta, rivolto a Bessa verso l'interno*]   8
Moa, moa, no me di' altro. [*A parte, tra sé*] Cancaro, a' m'he pensò de far la bela noela al vegio. A' son pur venturin, a' in guagnerè mi de sta noela, e sí a' me darè piasere. La m'ha donò sto bel fazoleto. [*Lo spiega, tenendolo tra le mani*] O fazoleto, fazoleto, te serè cason che 'l me tirerà sempre mé el cuore a colie che me te ha dò. A' me sborezerè con ti, con a' no la possa aver ela.

[*Sogguarda i due forestieri*] Chi cancaro—a' son pur   9
aliegro!—chi cancaro è costoro? Spagnaruoli? I m'ha cossí çiera de quel che ha comprò mia madona, de no esser compí d'i so limbri. A' i vuò pur saluare. [*Saluta rispettosamente Ginevra*] Sanitè, missier signore.

GINEVRA. Ben possi star, fratello. Averesti tu veduto tre   10
giovani, già stati prigioni de' corsalli, e vano cercando chi li rescuota? E entrano nelle case delle gentildonne, pregando che voglino riscuoterli, et essi a' servigii suoi si aconciariano?

RUZANTE. Qui pigè preson de' Turchi? Sí, sí, a' gi he   11
vezú zà un pezato. El ghe n'è un che sa cossí ben cosire e taiare...

GINEVRA. Quelli, dico io. Saprestimegli insegnare?   12
Uno de loro è mio fratello, e sono venuto per riscuoterlo.

RUZANTE. El ghe n'è un vostro frelo? Dîme mo a mi   13
qual l'è, fuossi ve saverègie meter su la via che a' 'l caterí.

Oh, someone is coming out of that house; perhaps he'll be able to inform us. [*To Ruzante, who is just coming out of Doralice's house*] Ho, you there.

SCENE TWO

Ruzante, Ginevra, and Ghitta

RUZANTE. [*on the threshold, turned to Bessa within*] Go on, go on, say no more. [*Aside, to himself*] Damn, I thought of a good trick to pull on the old man. The luck of it is that I'll make a good profit from this story and I'll have some fun. She gave me this beautiful kerchief. [*He unfolds it, holding it up in both hands*]. Oh, kerchief, kerchief, you'll always make my heart pound for the girl who gave you to me. I'll play with you when I can't have her.

[*He notices two strangers*]. Who the devil—I'm feeling chipper!—who the devil are they? Spaniards? They have the same pallor as the chap my mistress paid for, not furnished with every member. I'll say hello. [*He greets Ginevra respectfully*]. Good health, sir.

GINEVRA. Well met, brother. Might you have seen three youths who were once taken prisoners by corsairs and now are looking for someone to ransom them? They are visiting ladies at their homes asking for someone to pay their ransom in exchange for their services.

RUZANTE. Those Turkish prisoners? Yes, yes, I saw them a while ago. One of them knows how to sew and cut . . .

GINEVRA. They are the very ones I mean. Could you direct me to them? One of them is my brother, and I've come to pay his ransom.

RUZANTE. Your brother? Tell me which one he is; I may be able to set you on your way to finding him.

GINEVRA. Egli è il piú picolo di persona, con bellissimo 14
aspetto umano, reverente; gli atti suoi sonno pieni di alcune gentileze, che par tuto amore, tuto legiadria.

RUZANTE. Sí, sí, un tal scarmeto, smenueto, biancheto, 15
coluorío con è una rava in lo volto, con du ocieti che
par stele a çimegare... Sí, sí, l'è elo, sí.

GINEVRA. Egli è piú piciol di persona de gli altri dui, 16
ma è piú grande di grazia e di beltà.

RUZANTE. L'ha un àere tofoloto. Sí, l'è quelo, sí, sí. 17

GINEVRA. Come ne hai domestichezza, che ne sei cossí 18
ben informato? Conoscilo tu?

RUZANTE. Poh, s'a' 'l cognosso! La mia parona, sí, la 19
mia parona, l'ha rescosso ela, che la 'l vol tegnire serviore
a pè d'ela sempre, perché el sa cossí ben cosire e taiare,
conzar scufie, gonele de sea; sí el me paron ghe l'ha rescovú, elo. E sí è vostro frelo, quelo?

GINEVRA. Egli è quello. [A parte] Ahi, sventurata me, 20
costei è stata piú saggia e piú presta di me!

GHITTA. [piano, a parte] Di' piú saggio e piú presto. 21
Dirai di me, che mi bucina el cervello.

GINEVRA. [piano, a Ghitta] Eh, che non so piú che mi 22
dire... Io mi voglio scoprire a costui, ché altro rimedio
non ci veggio. L'amor deve esser come se dice in proverbio, che la piaga si deve portar sopra la palma de la
mano. Io me gli voglio scoprire.

GHITTA. Fa' tu, come ti piace.

RUZANTE. [piano, tra sé] A' no intendo. Mo sta' a dar 23
mente, te no verè che questa vol esser una bona noela
per mi? Tasi pure.

GINEVRA. [a Ruzante] Giovene, poiché mi sei stato 24
cossí cortese, io te voglio palesare un mio secreto. E oltra
di ciò, pregarti che aiuto o consiglio mi doni, perché io,

GINEVRA. He's the smallest in stature, with a very fair and civil appearance, respectful; his movements are so filled with every grace that he seems all love, all loveliness.

RUZANTE. Yes, yes, one such pipsqueak, tiny, pale, a face the color of a turnip, with two eyes blinking like stars . . . yes, yes, he's the one, yes.

GINEVRA. He's smaller in stature than the other two, but larger in grace and beauty.

RUZANTE. He has a puffed-up air. Yes, he's the one, yes, yes.

GINEVRA. How do you know about him, how do you come to be so well informed? Are you acquainted with him?

RUZANTE. Poh, am I acquainted with him! My mistress, yes, my mistress paid his ransom, and she wants to keep him by her side all the time because he can sew and cut, make caps and silken petticoats . . . yes, my master ransomed him for her. And he is your brother, that one?

GINEVRA. That is he. [*Aside*] Alas, hapless am I. This woman has been wiser and quicker than I.

GHITTA. [*quietly, aside*] Wiser and quicker. You'll be saying that I'm known for my brains.

GINEVRA. [*quietly, to Ghitta*] Oh, I no longer know what to say . . . I'll discover myself to this man, for I see no other remedy. Love must do as in the proverb that says to wear your heart on your sleeve. I shall tell him who I am.

GHITTA. Do as you like.

RUZANTE. [*quietly, to himself*] I don't understand. But pay attention and you'll see if there isn't a good plot in it for me. Quiet, please.

GINEVRA. [*to Ruzante*] Young man, as you have been so courteous to me, I wish to reveal my secret to you. Furthermore, I pray you give me aid or counsel, and I

de danari e care gioie, che meco mi atrovo, te ne farò
quella parte, che ti contentarai.

RUZANTE. Mo ontiera, pur che a' possa... Ma de qui   25
de in bona fe', sí, perché no? Se Diè m'ai', sí, sí, ben, mi,
che a' ve airè. A' son stò an mi per lo mondo, a' sè ben
che cossa è essere in luogo, don' no se cognosse negun.
Di' pure.

GINEVRA. [a bassa voce, accostandoglisi] Io son donna, e   26
son anconitana, vedoa, rica e inamorata.

RUZANTE. [sorpreso] Vu a' si' una femena? Vu? Poh, el   27
no gh'è cuore che a' no diesse che a' fossè un omo, a
vêrve de drio in le spale; e denanzo, a' parí un de sti
putacion, a muò scolaro.

GINEVRA. Ascolta: amor mi ha guidato cossí. Capito-   28
rono questi giovani in Ancona, né prima vidi colui, che
dici che ha riscosso la patrona tua, che di lui ferventemente m'inamorai. E non che picola quantità de dinari
averia speso per riscuoterlo, ma lo avanzo de le mie fa-
cultadi, che vagliono pur da vinticinque in trenta millia
fiorini d'oro. Ma, per la freta che ebbe il mercatante di
partirse, avene che [non] potei piú vederlo che quella
prima volta. E intesi che verso Vinegia avea drito il suo
camino; onde io disposi di doverlo seguire, e postami,
con gran quantità di moneta in borsa, sopra un piciol
legneto, li sequitai in questo abito come mi vedi, e con
questa mia sola fante. E gionta a Vinegia, intesi essi in
questa famosa città di Padoa esser pervenuti, drieto me
li son condota, credendo fermamente riavere il mio
amante. Il che vedi ben come mi è tornato falace; onde
non creggio mai piú viver lieta, ma sempre [sconso-
lata]... [e piange].

RUZANTE. [commosso] Orbéntena, quel che no fa un   29
inamorò, no 'l fara' gnan un soldò. A quanto prígolo a'
ve si' metú, vu povereta! An mi, al sangue del cancaro,
a' no sè con supia vivo, ch'a' no supia stò mazò morto
diese fiè. Quando iera inamorò, andasea tuto 'l dí, de

will share to your satisfaction the money and precious jewels I am carrying.

RUZANTE. Why, gladly, if I am able . . . Why, certainly, in good faith, yes, why not? With the Lord's help yes, yes, certainly I will help you. I've been around in the world myself and I know what it's like to be in a place where you don't know anyone. Tell me, by all means.

GINEVRA. [*in a low voice, drawing close to him*] I am a woman from Ancona, a widow, rich, and in love.

RUZANTE. [*surprised*] You are female? You? Poh, there's not a soul that would say you were not a man, looking at your shoulders from the back, and from the front you look like one of those young rascals, like a student.

GINEVRA. Hear me out: love has been my guide. These youths arrived in Ancona and no sooner did I see him, the one you say your mistress ransomed, than I fell passionately in love. And no mere sum of money would I have paid to ransom him, but the rest of my estate, which is worth twenty-five to thirty thousand gold florins. Yet, because the merchant was in a hurry to leave I was unable to see him again after that first time. I heard that he had set his course for Venice, whereupon I resolved that I had to follow him, so setting out on a small bark with a large sum of money in my purse, I followed them, dressed in this outfit, as you see me, with this one maidservant. When I reached Venice I heard that they had gone on to this famous city of Padua and I followed after them, firmly resolved to have my beloved back again. But you see how wrong I was in that matter; wherefore I think I shall never again live happily, but be forever disconsolate . . . [*She weeps*].

RUZANTE. [*touched*] Well now, what a lover will do not even a soldier would. You've risked so much danger, you poor girl! I, too, blasted blood, don't know how I am alive, how I have not been slain dead ten times. When I was in love I used to wander all day and night

note, per segrè,[1] a' dormía soto nogare, che no sè che no
supia inorcò, insperitò, che no abie trenta meiara de
spiriti adosso! No pianzí, povereta, no ve destruzí, ch'a'
v'imprometo de far che a' l'averí. Stè de bona vuogia.

GINEVRA. Oh, volesselo Idio! Che oltre quello che   30
spenderei per riscuoterlo, te faria uno presente a te di
altra tanta quantità.

RUZANTE. Andè, che inchina damò a' me ubigo squase   31
che a' l'averí. In che luogo stèu?

GINEVRA. Alla Osteria de la Torre è la stanzia nostra.   32
Vieni, e dicinerai con esso nui, e imparerai la stancia. Ma
dimi, come li dirai? Che fictione troverai, che la tua madonna non se ne acorga?

RUZANTE. A' ve dirè, mi: elo no ghe sta vontiera. A'   33
ghe favelerè a elo, e sí a' ghe dirè... Laghè pur far a mi.
Tornè de chivelòndena fina un pezato, che a' ve aspiterè
e sí a' ve saverè dire con averè fato. Una fià, cherzo fremamen da far ch'a' l'averí. A' ve zuro che a' m'aí tuto
conturbolò el magon... Se foessè altra ca vu, a' no 'l farae
miga per un'altra, vi'; mo perché a' si' vignú d'oltra el
mare, a' me fé pecò.

GINEVRA. Eh, falo di grazia, ti priego, ché la mia vita   34
in questo ponto dimora!

RUZANTE. Muora? A' no vuò che 'l muora negun.   35
Andè, e tornè de chivelòndena fina un pezato, che a'
spiero che a' ve darè bone noele.

GINEVRA. Anderò, dunque.

GHITTA. Andiamo, madonna, sí, poiché cossí larga-   36
mente ti promete.

[*Escono entrambe*].

RUZANTE. Moa, andè pure. [*Solo*] Al sangue del can-   37
caro, el me ven pur le gran venture. A' scaperè su ste
puoche de brombete de suoldi an da st'altra. Mo el no
besogna ch'a' ghe dighe che la supia una femena, ché a'
no farae gnente.

through graveyards and sleep beneath nut trees; I don't know how I'm not haunted, bewitched, why I don't have thirty thousand ghosts at my back! Don't cry, poor girl, don't waste away. I promise I'll get him for you. Be of good cheer.

GINEVRA. Oh, may the Lord will it so! Then in addition to whatever I spend to ransom him, I will make you a gift of the same amount.

RUZANTE. Go, henceforth I am busy arranging for you to have him. Where are you staying?

GINEVRA. The Inn of the Tower is our lodging. Come dine with us and you will learn its location. But tell me, what will you say to him? What fiction will you invent so that your mistress is not aware of it?

RUZANTE. I must tell you: he's not happy with us. I'll speak to him and I'll say . . . Leave it to me. Come back to this spot in a little while; I'll wait for you and I'll let you know what I've arranged. Once more, I am positive that I can get him for you. I swear, you've made my stomach turn over . . . If it were for anyone else, I wouldn't do it, but because you've come from across the sea, I feel sorry for you.

GINEVRA. Ah, please do it, please. I beseech you, for my life depends on it!

RUZANTE. She may die? I don't want anyone to die. Go and come back to this spot in a little while when I expect to give you good news.

GINEVRA. Then I shall go.

GHITTA. Let's go, my lady, indeed, since he promises you so generously.

[*They both leave*].

RUZANTE. Go, please go. [*Alone*] Blasted blood, great adventures just come my way. I'll pick up a few plums of coin from this young woman. But I mustn't tell her we're dealing with a female or there'll be nothing doing.

Al sangue de mi, an st'altra farà de quele de la mia   38
parona. Con la crerà meter le man a la pria da gussare, la
caterà el coaro vuo'. A' no cherzo che 'l foesse la pí bela
fiaba al mondo de questa. Vaga pure al bordelo, questi
che fa le comierie! I dise po che l'amore no fa fare. Te
par che st'altra, che è una femena, supia vegnúa d'oltra
el mare in qua, perché? Per amore. Orbéntena, a' he sentío dire che l'amore è un putato, e che 'l va con gi uoci
abindè, e che l'ha le ale; altri dise che l'è un putatuolo
desordenò. E mi a' dighe, e sí a' tegno fremamen, e de
questo a' vora' contrastare con quanti sletràn imparè mé
letra, se 'l foesse ben Sòstene² bonamen, che Amore no
è altro che potinzia e desidierio,³ e che un tira l'altro.

Te pàrsele brombe tirar una femena d'oltra el mare in   39
qua? E po drio a n'altra femena? Che te pàrsestre? On' se
aldí mé dire che una vaca andesse drio a n'altra vaca per
amore, né na scroa drio a n'altra scroa, né na piegora drio
a n'altra piegora? Èlo tirare mo? Èla potinzia? Mo dasché
la va da tirare e da poere, a' vorò vêre an mi s'a' posso
tirare sti puo' de beziti.

A la fe' d'omo, el besogna che supia perd'omo. Una   40
fià la mia parona, pur che l'abia i suò dinari, a' cherzo
che de punti e de strapunti la supia pí stufa, che n'è can
de carogna. [*Esce*].

SCENA TERZA

TANCREDI e TEODORO

TANCREDI. Teodoro, cortesi, magnifici e liberali gen-   41
tiluomeni ha questa città per certo. Come hanno cortese-
mente dato a noi li denari per potersi liberare, e poi di-
tone che il stare nelle case loro è a piacer nostro! Mai
non mi uscirà di mente tanto beneficio. Io li sarò tenuto
e obrigato fino alla morte.

By my blood, this woman is probably making the same mistake as my mistress. When she thinks she's putting her hand to the honing stone, she'll find the container empty. There's never been a better tale than this. To the brothels with them—those comic writers! They say love doesn't make things happen. Why do you think this woman, a female, has come here from across the sea? Why? For love. I've heard that love is a little boy with blindfolded eyes and wings; others say he is a fickle child. I say, and I hold it for certain, and I would argue the point with as many scholars as ever studied letters, if it were Aristotle himself, that Love is none other than potency and desire, one attracting the other.

Do you think plums attracted a woman from across the sea to here? And after another woman at that! What do you make of it? Did you ever hear of a cow going after another cow for love, or a sow after another sow, or a sheep after another sheep? Is that attraction? Is that potency? But between pulling and pushing I'll see if I can attract myself a piece of change.

In faith, I must be brave. As far as my mistress is concerned, as long as she gets her money back, I think she's fed up with points and stitches, like a dog with carrion. [*He exits*].

SCENE THREE

TANCREDI and TEODORO

TANCREDI. Teodoro, the gentlemen in this city are certainly courteous, splendid, and generous. How kindly they have given money for us to regain our freedom, and then they invited us to stay in their homes at our pleasure! Never will I forget their beneficence. I shall remain beholden and obliged to them until death.

TEODORO. Io ho sempre udito lodare questa cità per 42
bella cità, ma invero le persone che l'abitano la fano
parer molto piú bella. Chi sarà quel'ingrato, che non
abia fin che viva sempre tanto beneficio avanti gli ochi?
Io, per me, ovunque mi sia, sempre ne tenirò conto,
come di cossa degna di eterna memoria.

Deh, Tancredi, vogliam nui partirci, se non ritro- 43
viamo Gismondo? Oh, gran fallo sarebbe cossí dolce
compagno lasciare, ancora che non sia de la nostra cità.

TANCREDI. Anci voglio che lo rimeniamo con noi, se 44
egli vorà venire. E ti voglio dir piú: che, se egli fusse
femina, mi sarei di lui inamorato ardentissimamente,
tanto mi hanno sempre piaciuti gli laudevoli costumi
suoi. E parmi, dippoi che siamo separati da lui, che io
abia meno una parte dil core. Che si sia, non lo so io, né
onde si venga.

TEODORO. Oh, egli aviene che in questa miseria, in 45
questa tristicia, siamo fatti tuta tre compagni, e meglio si
giongono i pet[t]i de amicizia ne le calamitadi, ne' disaggi, che ne li comodi e piaceri.

Ma io mi sento nel core un non so che, che mi ralegra 46
tuto, e par che mi prometa grandissima alegreza. Cerchiamo, di grazia, Gismondo, andiamo a lo albergo di
quella gentildonna che lo riscatò.

TANCREDI. Andiamo.

[*Escono*].

SCENA QUARTA

GINEVRA e GHITTA

GINEVRA. Eh, non mi confortare, çhe so ben io che 47
spero invano! Credi tu che quella gentildonna se lo abia
rescosso per lasiarlo poi, perché io el riabia? Eh, che
speranze frali son queste!

TEODORO. I've always heard this city praised for its beauty, but truly, the people who live here make it even more beautiful. Who is so ungrateful that he would not hold such kindness before his eyes so long as he lives. As for me, wherever I may be, I will always be mindful of it as worthy of eternal memory.

But Tancredi, shall we two go hence without finding Gismondo? Oh, what a pity it would be to leave so sweet a companion behind, even though he's not from our hometown.

TANCREDI. On the contrary, I want to take him back with us if he's willing to come. And I'll tell you something else: if he were a woman, I would be ardently in love with him, so much have his laudable ways always pleased me. Why, I feel that in the time we've been separated from him I lack a bit of my heart. What it may mean, I do not know, nor what makes it happen.

TEODORO. Oh, it's to be expected that in this misery and sorrow we three have become comrades; hearts are better joined in friendship by calamities and privations than by comforts and pleasures.

But I feel in my heart something that gladdens me utterly and seems to promise me very great joy. Please, let us search for Gismondo; let's go to the lodgings of that gentle lady who ransomed him.

TANCREDI. Let's go.

[*They exit*].

SCENE FOUR

GINEVRA and GHITTA

GINEVRA. Ah, comfort me not, for well do I know that I hope in vain! Do you think that gentlewoman paid his ransom only to let him go so I might have him back? Ah, what frail hopes these are!

GHITTA. Colui deve pur aver fondata la sua opinione 48
sopra qualche cossa. Chi pò saper li cori delle persone?
Forse non l'ama ella tanto ferventemente come l'ami tu.

GINEVRA. Eh, chi non l'ama, che lo abi una volta ve- 49
duto, cregio che non deve amare sé stesso! Parti che
quelle siano bellezze da non amare? Anci son io certis-
sima che quella, piú aventurosa di me, non mai li deb-
bia levar le brazia dal collo, e in casa e fuore non li si
deba levar mai da presso. Adesso se lo debbe vanegiare,
adesso se lo abracia, adesso li dice che egli è il suo core,
la sua vita, la sua speranza, la sua colona, el suo con-
forto, adesso, adesso, sventurata me! Oh, fortuna crudel!
[*Sospira*].

GHITTA. Forse che 'l marito di lei, entrato in qualche 50
gelosia, non vorà che lo istia in casa. Chi pò saper tute le
cosse de questo mondo?

GINEVRA. Eh, amore non li insegnarà il modo di far 51
star cheto il marito? Non saperà ordir qualche sua favola,
qualche sua zancia? Quando il marito la cruziasse sopra
ciò, non saperà ella dire: «Che credete voi, ch'io sia
scessa de villani? Che voglia far copia di me a un schiavo?
Non mi avete già ricolta del fango! In mal ponto vi venni
in casa, per non esser mai lieta. Alla Croce de Idio, me-
ritareste che vi facesse pensar del vero, come fano de le
altre. Voi non eravate degno de mei fati». E che vòi che
li risponda il marito, se non che si tacia?

GHITTA. Tu te immagini gran cosse per certo.

GINEVRA. Io me imagino quello che facilmente po- 52
trebbe essere. Or torniamoci allo albergo. Costui non
ritornerà, oggi. Io saria andata da l'altro capo di questa
cità e ritornata.

GHITTA. [*scotendo il capo*] Forsi con el pensiero li saresti 53
andata. Non deve esser ancora per aventura gionto
a casa.

[*Escono*].

GHITTA. That man must have based his opinion on something. Who can know what's in a person's heart? Maybe she doesn't love him as passionately as you do.

GINEVRA. Anyone who does not love him, once she has seen him, cannot, I think, love herself. Do you suppose such beauty can go unloved? On the contrary, I am quite sure that she, more enterprising than I, never takes her arms from his neck, and whether at home or away, never lets him leave her side. Now she must be gushing, now she is embracing him; now she is saying he is her heart, her life, her hope, her support, her comfort, now, now, wretched me! Oh, cruel fortune! [*She sighs*].

GHITTA. Perhaps her husband has become jealous and doesn't want him in the house. Who can know everything in this world?

GINEVRA. Ah, will love not teach her a way to silence her husband? Won't she spin some tale, some tattle? When her husband takes her to task about it, won't she say: "Do you think I am descended from peasants? That I want to join myself to a slave? You didn't lift me up out of the mud! In an evil hour I came to your home, never to be happy. By God on the Cross, it would serve you right if I really gave you something to worry about, as other women do. You were never worthy of me." And how do you expect her husband to respond if not by keeping quiet?

GHITTA. You certainly have plenty of imagination.

GINEVRA. I am imagining what may well be happening. Now let us return to the inn. That man won't be back today. I could have been to one end of the city and back again.

GHITTA. [*shaking her head*] Perhaps you would have gone in your mind. He probably hasn't reached the house yet.

[*They exit*].

ATTO QUARTO

SCENA PRIMA

RUZANTE e GISMONDO, poi GINEVRA e GHITTA

RUZANTE. El dise che l'è d'oltra el mare, d'una tera che   1
ha lome a muò ste imagine che se depenze su le carte e
se ten apichè a i muri.

GISMONDO. Statue? Deve esser Capua.[1]   2

RUZANTE. No, cancaro, statole! De quele che porta qui   3
che ven da Loreto, el se ven an de lí via... De queste che
se avre e che se sera... Quando un vol biastemare, i dise:
«Te me farè catar l'anconeta»... De Anconeta.[2]

GISMONDO. De Ancona, deve esser.

RUZANTE. Sí, sí, sí, l'è ela. Mo ben, l'è de là, elo.   4

GISMONDO. Oh, quanto me incresse aver lassiata la   5
madonna tua! Io li avea posto già lo magior amore del
mondo. Ma dimi, ove abiam noi a trovare questo gentiluomo di Ancona?

RUZANTE. Chialò denanzo. O, se a' no 'l caterón, an-   6
darón a l'ostaria, ché 'l sta là, elo. Cancaro, l'è un om da
ben, viu. El me ha voiú menar, ch'a' disnesse con elo, el
me ha [a]n promesso de donarme dinari, se fasea che 'l
ve favelesse.

GISMONDO. [*pensieroso*] De Ancona? Chi puote esser   7
costui? Se egli fusse femina, io mi dubiterei che egli fusse
in quel medesmo eror che pocco dinanzi era la patrona
tua. Ma, essendo uomo, e di Ancona, esser potrà che
averà tolto un per l'altro.

RUZANTE. In falo? No, cancaro, el me ha pur dè i con-   8
trasigni tuti, a comuò sii fato. Io no pò star ch'i no
sponte. [*Entrano in quella Ginevra e Ghitta*]. Vîgi, vîgi, gi
è quisti. [*Si avvicina a Ginevra e le parla, mentre Gismondo-*

ACT FOUR

SCENE ONE

RUZANTE and GISMONDO, then GINEVRA and GHITTA

RUZANTE. He says he's from abroad, from a place with a name that sounds like those painted images they attach to the wall.

GISMONDO. Statues? It must be Capua.

RUZANTE. No, damn it, not statues! Those things people bring here when they come from Loreto . . . they make them there too . . . those things that open and shut . . . When someone curses, he says: "You'll make me knock down the altar icon" . . . from Icona.

GISMONDO. It must be Ancona.

RUZANTE. Yes, yes, yes, that's it. Right, that's where he's from.

GISMONDO. Oh, how sorry I am to have left your mistress! I had already placed in her all the love in the world. But tell me, where are we to find this gentleman from Ancona?

RUZANTE. Here ahead. Or if we don't find him we'll go to the inn where he's staying. Blast it, he's a decent fellow. He wanted me to go there to dine with him, and he promised to give me some money if I arranged for him to speak to you.

GISMONDO. [*thoughtful*] From Ancona? Who can it be? If it were a woman I'd suspect she was making the same mistake your mistress made a little earlier. But as he is a man, and from Ancona, he may have mistaken me for someone else.

RUZANTE. Mistake? No, the pox, he described your distinguishing features to me. It's impossible they don't match. [*Ginevra and Ghitta enter*]. Look, look, here they are. [*He approaches Ginevra and speaks to her while Gis-*

Isotta resta in disparte] Ve 'l dissi ch'a' ve 'l menerave? La mia parona no vol dinari, la gh'ha dò libertè che 'l vaga on' el vò elo. Andè mo in bonora tuti. Mi a' he priessia, a' no vuò pí star co vu, a' vuò andare. S'a' me volí dar gnente, déme. [*Stende la mano*].

GINEVRA. Alla tua patrona e a te sarò sempre obrigato.   9
Ma dove vòi gire? Non vòi venire a l'albergo, e dicinerai con noi?

RUZANTE. Missier no, missier no, a' he priessia.   10

GINEVRA. [*offrendogli una piccola borsa di denaro*] Se re-   11
maner non vòi, piglia adonque questi, e te ne farai un giupone e un paio di calce, e quelle per amor mio porterai.

RUZANTE. [*intascandola*] A' i torè, e sí a' me le farè an a   12
la divisa, le calçe.³ Moa, stè con Dio. Co' a' vegne a Loreto, a' ve vegnerè ben a catare. [*Allontanandosi, passa vicino a Gismondo, che lo interroga*].

GISMONDO. Tu te ne vai, Rugiante?   13

RUZANTE. Mo sí, mi, a' vago.

GISMONDO. Saluterai el patron per parte mia.   14

RUZANTE. Moa, moa, sí, sí. [*A parte*] A' me vuò snetare   15
presto, inanzo che i se acorza che le supia femene tute do. A' n'he fato un s-ciapeto de do vache, e tre con la massara; a' no sè mo chi sarà el toro. [*Esce*].

SCENA SECONDA

GISMONDO, GINEVRA e GHITTA

GISMONDO. [*a Ginevra*] Gentiluomo, parmi di avervi   16
altrove veduto, e ho pensato e penso, e finalmente non posso ricordarmi dove. Però ditemi, di grazia, chi siete, e la cagione che vi fa cercar di me.

GINEVRA. Sapiate, grazioso giovene, che io sopra tute   17
le cosse del mondo vi amo, né altro che l'amor che vi

mondo / Isotta stands aside]. Didn't I tell you I'd bring him to you? My mistress doesn't want any money; she has given him liberty to go wherever he wants. Let's all be quickly on our way. I'm in a hurry, I can't stay here with you any longer, I have to go. If you have anything for me, let me have it. [*He holds out his hand*].

GINEVRA. I am obliged'to you and to your mistress forever. But where are you going? Don't you want to come to the inn and sup with us?

RUZANTE. No sir, sir, no. I'm in a hurry.

GINEVRA. [*offering him a money purse*] If you don't want to stay, take this, and you can have a greatcoat made, and a pair of hose, and wear them with my love.

RUZANTE. [*putting the purse in his pocket*] I'll take it, and I'll even have a decoration on the hose. Well, God be with you. When I come to Loreto, I'll look you up. [*Leaving, he passes by Gismondo, who asks him*]

GISMONDO. Are you leaving, Ruzante?

RUZANTE. Yes, I'm on my way.

GISMONDO. Give my regards to your master.

RUZANTE. Why yes, certainly, yes. [*Aside*] I'll beat it in a hurry before they realize that they are both women. I've made a herd of two cows, three with the maid; I don't know who'll be the bull. [*He exits*].

SCENE TWO

GISMONDO, GINEVRA, and GHITTA

GISMONDO. [*to Ginevra*] Gentle sir, I feel as though I've seen you somewhere else, and I've thought and thought, still I cannot remember where. So tell me, please, who you are, and why you have sought me out.

GINEVRA. Fair youth, know that above all things in the world, I love you, nor has anything but my love for you

porto mi ha condota, femina e peregrina, a sequitarvi in questo abito, come Amor con suo consiglio me ha insegnato. Io son donna, e in Gagieta¹ nata; ma, per alcun caso, che longo saria a ricontare, mi fugi' dal mio patre, e in Ancona divieni moglie de un richissimo giovene, il quale, morendo, non è ancor finito l'anno, mi lasciò di tute le cosse sue richissima posseditrice et erede. Or advene, quando voi capitaste in Ancona, che vi vidi; né prima affissai gli ochi mei ne la luce de[gli] ochi vostri, che mi piaquero somamente, insiemme con le legiadre fatece vostre; e una e un'altra volta riguardandovi, mi pareva, da non so che cossa occulta mossa, che altre volte vi avesse similmente veduto, e come carissimo amico amato. E tanto si formò in me questo pensiero, che o per sogno credeva avervi altre volte veduto e amato, o che un'altra volta fussemo stati al mondo insiemme, se esser può; e da questo pensiero naque in me un cossí subito e ardentissimo amore, in modo che mi disposi, se per oro si potesse riavervi, non risparmiar denari. E mentre cercava modo di parlarvi, e con il mercatante, avene che con gran presteza vi partiste: perciò piú crebbe lo amore in me, che che se ne avenisse, [di] sequirvi e tanto operare, che o con furto, o con denari, o con promesse, vi ritornasse in libertà, e dippoi di me farvi signore. Il che mi è successo meglio di quello mi pensai; onde ringrazio Idio, e apresso vi prego che di me vogliate aver pietade, e de lo amor vostro vogliate farmi cortese dono, come io di me e de le cosse mie vi facio, e voglio siate signore. E benché de lo amor mio sia stato non legier segno lo avervi sequito, pur, per piú vostra sicurtà, in quello che piú a grado vi sia mi comandareti, che mi avereti sempre pronta ad obedirvi.

GISMONDO. [*sospira*] Eh, eh, ehimè!

GINEVRA. Ohimè, come sospiraste voi! Vi sono forse 18 nogliose le parole mie? Lo amor mio non vi è a grado?

persuaded me, a woman and pilgrim, to follow you dressed in this way as Love's counsel taught me. I am a woman, born in Gaeta; but because of circumstances too long to relate, I ran away from my father and in Ancona I became the wife of a very rich young man, who died less than a year ago, leaving me the wealthy proprietress and heir of all he possessed. When you landed in Ancona I happened to see you there, and no sooner did my eyes light upon yours than I liked them exceedingly, as well as your lovely features, and after seeing you once, and then again, I felt moved as if by something occult, as if I had seen you other times as well, as a very dear beloved friend. And this thought grew in me until I believed either that I had seen and loved you once in a dream, or that we had been in the world together at some other time, if such a thing is possible; and out of this thought a sudden blazing love arose in me, whereupon I decided that if gold could bring you back, I would not spare any expense. But while I was trying to find a way to speak with you and the merchant, in great haste you departed; then all the more did my love increase, and I resolved that come what may I would follow you and do anything, whether by theft or money or promises, to restore your liberty and make you my lord. All of which has succeeded better than I expected; and I thank God for it, and I pray you to have pity on me and make me the courteous gift of your love as I make you of myself and of what belongs to me, and be my lord. Even though my having followed you here is no light token of my love, still for your greater assurance you may command me in whatever pleases you most and you will have me ever ready to obey.

GISMONDO. [*sighs*] Oh, oh, alas!

GINEVRA. Alack, how you sighed! Are my words disturbing? Do you not welcome my love?

GISMONDO. Quando non mi fusse a grado lo amor vostro, madonna, né anco la vita mia istessa mi potria esser a grado. Ma sospirai d'altro.

GINEVRA. Perché sospiraste voi?

GISMONDO. Per la recordazione che avete fato di 19 Gaieta. Ma, di grazia, non mi negate ch'io sapia chi fu el padre vostro, poiché in Gaieta sète nata.

GINEVRA. Messer Gabrioto de gli Onesti fu il padre 20 mio, e la madre mia mona Dionora di Neri.²

GISMONDO. Ebbe il padre vostro piú figliuoli o figliuole di voi?

GINEVRA. Sí, ebbe. Un'altra figliuola ci rimase, poi che 21 da lui mi fugi' in Ancona. E intesi quella da un uomo d'arme esser stata levata e guidata via. Dove si capitasse, né il padre né io abiamo mai potuto risapere; per il che per morta è stata pianta.

GISMONDO. Conossereste voi la sorella vostra, se viva 22 la vedeste?

GINEVRA. Se la età non l'avesse transformata dagli anni 23 puerili, io mi cregio di tenir di lei tal rememorazione, che facilmente la conoscerei.

GISMONDO. Poniamo che la ritrovaste. Quanto vi saria 24 a caro?

GINEVRA. Quanto che aquistar la grazia vostra, signor 25 mio caro, che desidero sopra tute le cosse del mondo. Però che, trovandola, parerà avenir a me come aviene a un peregrino, che solo per un strano diserto camine, e ritrove un suo carissimo amico; che, quanto men sperava di trovarlo, tanto piú si ralegra. Perché io son senza alcuno di mei parenti o coniunti al mondo, e mi posso dir sola.

GISMONDO. Non mi maraveglio che, da celata virtú 26 mossa, cossí grande e subito amor me abiate posto: però che el sangue vostro e le carne vostre istesse amate. Io sono la vostra isventurata sorella Isota, da voi come morta pianta, otto anni peregrina andata e tre schiava

GISMONDO. If your love were not welcome, my lady, then neither would my life itself be welcome. I sighed because of something else.

GINEVRA. Why did you sigh?

GISMONDO. Because you brought back a memory of Gaeta. Please, permit me to know who your father was, as you were born in Gaeta.

GINEVRA. Master Gabrioto of the Onesti family was my father, and my mother was Lady Dionora of the Neri family.

GISMONDO. Did your father have any sons or daughters other than yourself?

GINEVRA. Yes, he did. Another daughter remained there after I fled to Ancona. I heard that she was abducted by a man of arms and taken away. Where she arrived neither our father nor I ever learned, so she was mourned for dead.

GISMONDO. Would you recognize your sister if you saw her alive?

GINEVRA. If age has not transformed her since our childhood years, I believe that my memory of her is such that I would recognize her easily.

GISMONDO. Let's say that you found her. How precious would she be to you?

GINEVRA. As much as acquiring your favor, my precious sir, which I desire more than anything in the world. If I found her I would feel like a pilgrim walking alone through a strange wilderness who discovers a very dear friend, and the less hope he had of finding him, that much more does he rejoice; for having no relatives or in-laws in the world, I must say I am alone.

GISMONDO. I am not surprised that, stirred by a secret force, you felt so great and sudden a love for me, for it is your own flesh and blood that you love. I am your hapless sister, Isotta, whom you mourned for dead; I have been a wanderer for eight years and for three years a

stata. Lodato Idio, che inanzi la mia morte mi vi fa vedere, e in lieto stato ritrovarvi!

[*Le due sorelle si gettano le braccia al collo*].

GHITTA. [*a parte*] A che è riuscito lo amor de mia ma- 27
donna, in una sua sorella? Che nuovo caso è questo? Chi
racontasse questo esser in Padoa intervenuto, ne saria re-
putato bugiardo. E pur è cossí in effeto.

GINEVRA. Ahi, dolcissima sorella, a gran fatica ritengo 28
le lacrime per tenereza! Andiamo allo albergo, ove re-
contaremo piú ad agio le nostre sventure, e senza rispeto.
Oh, quanto di alegreza mi è agionta, quanto spero di
menar lo avanzo di mia vita lieta, con cossí dolce compagnia come tu! Averò con cui partir li affanni e li piaceri, che mi porgerà la fortuna.

[*Ginevra e Gismondo-Isotta escono tenendosi teneramente
abbracciate*].

GHITTA. Io mi maraveglia[va] ben che quella gentil- 29
donna, che lo aveva fato riscuotere, cossí facilmente lo
avesse licenziato. Ma ora mi acorgo: perché ella non avea
ritrovato el gambo al finochio. [*Esce al seguito delle due
signore*].

SCENA TERZA

SIER TOMAO e RUZANTE

SIER TOMAO. [*solo, uscendo di casa*] Co' le cosse no va a 30
so voia, sto diavolo de sta mia moier trazerave el mondo
in aqua, se la lo avesse in man. Perché l'ha trovao che
colie che la credeva che fosse un omo, sè una femena, da
desperazion la l'ha licençiao senza danari. [*Scuote il capo,
seccato*].

El me recresse pí de essa, che no fa d'i danari. El me 31
giera vegnúo la ventura in casa, e la fortuna no ha vo-
lesto che me ghe abia trovao; ché mai no la lassava par-

slave. Praised be God for letting me see you before I die and for finding you in happy circumstances!

[*The two sisters embrace*].

GHITTA. [*aside*] Has my lady's love turned out to be her sister? What new matter is this? Anyone who said this had happened in Padua would be called a liar. Yet it's really so.

GINEVRA. Ah, sweetest sister, with great effort I hold back tears of tenderness! Let us go to the inn, where we will recount our misadventures more comfortably and without restraint. Oh, what joy overtakes me, how happily I hope to live the rest of my life with so sweet a companion as you! I will have someone with whom to share whatever afflictions and pleasures fortune may bring.

[*Ginevra and Gismondo/Isotta exit tenderly, arm in arm*].

GHITTA. I was amazed that the gentlewoman who had ransomed him dismissed him so easily. But now I understand; she found the fennel lacked a stem. [*She exits following the two ladies*].

SCENE THREE

SIER TOMAO and RUZANTE

SIER TOMAO. [*alone, coming out of his house*] When things don't go her way that devil wife of mine would throw the world into the sea if she could lift it in her hand. When she found out that the person she thought was male is female, in her dejection she let her go without getting her money back. [*He shakes his head, annoyed*].

I feel worse about the girl than for the money. Lady luck came to my house, but fortune didn't want her to find me home; I'd never have let her go. I could have

tir. E' me averave sborao con essa, talvolta, de sto mio inamoramento...

Orsú, pazienzia, vegnisse almanco costú. El sè tanto pegro...

RUZANTE. [*esce dalla casa di Doralice, e parla con Bessa* 32 *verso l'interno*] Che, ch'a' no donesse via el fazoleto? A' donerè inanzo via no so che! N'abiè paura de questo. Stè con Dio. [*Chiude l'uscio*] Andarón tuti du da ele, stasera, tondoron, dorin, dorin... [*Balla*] Al sangue del cancaro! La m'ha basò, che me vò lecare sta massela, don' la m'ha basò, con la lengua... [*Fa il lazzo*] Uh, uh, o boca melata, o man tofolote che m'ha tocò sta man, o saoreto pí lioso ca n'è na speçia... Uh, uh, cancaro, a' uolo tuto, inchina le scarpe me uole! [*Si annusa lungo il corpo, e starnutisce*] Ehí, ehí!...

SIER TOMAO. Èstu ti, Ruzante? An, a chi digo mi? 33

RUZANTE. Missier sí, missier sí, a' son mi, cancaro è 34 ch'a' son mi, e sí a' uolo da zilibeto, da sadabon. La me n'ha butà per adosso, sentíu? Inchiname' la schina, sen- tíu? [*Si fa annusare dal padrone*] La m'ha dò tanti pimenti, a' tegnía passè gi uoci, e sí la lagava fare. L'aéa una zu- cheta, e sí me butava tanta aqua. Nasè, le scarpe inchina me vuole... [*Solleva un piede fin sotto il naso del padrone*] Marco, Marco![1] Al sangue del cancaro...

SIER TOMAO. Sto sferdimento no me lassa sentir. Sta' 35 in pase, vie' zà, bestia, dime co' ti ha fato... [*Cerca di calmarlo*].

RUZANTE. Miegio ch'a' fesse mé in mia vita, e la meior 36 noela, per mi, che foesse mé.

SIER TOMAO. Ben, che cossa? Di' via, caro fio belo.

RUZANTE. La puta m'ha impromesso, ela, a mi! 37

SIER TOMAO. Va', diavolo! E' digo de mi. Co' hastu 38 fato de quele zanze?

expressed my feelings to her, sometimes, about this love of mine . . .

Now then, hold on, if he would just get here. He's so lazy . . .

RUZANTE. [*coming out of Doralice's house and speaking to Bessa within*] Don't give away this kerchief? I'd sooner give away, I don't know what! Have no fear of that. God be with you. [*He closes the door*]. We'll both go with them this evening, tondoron, dorin, dorin . . . [*He dances*]. Blasted blood! She kissed me; I'll lick my cheek where she kissed me, with my tongue . . . [*He licks his cheek*]. Oh, oh, oh honeyed mouth, supple hands that have touched this hand of mine, scent more aromatic than any spice . . . Uh, uh, blast it, I'm fragrant all over; even my shoes smell! [*He sniffs his body and sneezes*]. Ehi, ehi! . . .

SIER TOMAO. Is that you, Ruzante? To whom am I speaking?

RUZANTE. Yes, master, yes, master, it's me, blast it, it's me. I'm perfumed with musk, scented. She sprinkled it over me; smell? Even my backside, smell? [*He has his master sniff him*]. She gave me lots of perfume while I shut my eyes and let her do it. She has a little flask and she sprinkled water all over me. Smell, even my shoes are perfumed . . . [*He lifts a foot under his master's nose*]. Mark, Mark! blood of the canker . . .

SIER TOMAO. I can't smell with this cold. Calm down. Come here, dolt. Tell me how you've done . . . [*He tries to calm him*].

RUZANTE. Better than ever in my life; for me it's the best news I ever had.

SIER TOMAO. Well, what is it? Speak up, dear fair boy.

RUZANTE. The girl promised herself to me!

SIER TOMAO. Go on, the devil! I mean about me. What have you done about those slanders?

RUZANTE. Ben, missier. Poh, cancaro, se no foesse stò 39
mi, a' no fasivi mé gnente. Volívu altro? A' no volívi
gnian altro om ca mi, ché, se 'l no foesse mi... che mi,
m'intendo, la me ha obrigo, a mi. Volí altro? ch'a' sarí
servío.

SIER TOMAO. Ben, a che muodo? quando? in che 40
luogo?

RUZANTE. [*mettendosi in posa per raccontare*] Mo aldí, 41
missiere. Quando iera putato, che a' laghiè star de andar
con le biestie, che aéa quel can, che a' me 'l menava a
man, con a' ve dissi, a' scomenziè cossí a muò a trar a le
pute, che 'l no me trasea el cuore cossí al bestiame. A'
scomenziè andar a filò tute le sere, tal fià tre e quatro
megia lunzi, che 'l iera scuro con è una boca de lovo.

SIER TOMAO. Che diavolo de proposito sè questo? Che 42
ha a far la luna con i gambari? Te domando a che semo
del fato mio, ti me disi de to menar de bestiame, de to
filoi, de to merde!

RUZANTE. Prepuositi, bestiame. Aldí pure, tasí pure, gi 43
è buoni i prepuositi. Ascolteme, s'a' volí. [*Riattacca*] E sí,
con a' ve dego rivar de dire, de andar a filò, andasea tal
fià pí de oto megia. Ma sí! A' stemava cossí con farae a
magnar una nubià, o un brazelo... E po, con a' ve dego
rivar de dire, mo no catiège una note un lovo, che aéa
du oci che parea du candele, grande con è un gran
aseno?

SIER TOMAO. [*fremendo*] Pota, che ti me farà catar San 44
Marzo... Che diavolo ha a far lovi con el fato mio de mi?
E' voio parlar d'amor, e ti me rasoni de lovi, che manza
i cristiani.

RUZANTE. A' ve vuoio favelar an mi de amore, e del 45
vostro amor de vu. Mo aldí, s'a' volí.

SIER TOMAO. In mio preposito, in mia speçialitae 46
de mi?

RUZANTE. In prepuosito, in spetabilitè de vu. 47

RUZANTE. Very well, sir. Poh, pox, if it weren't for me you'd never do anything. Do you want anything else? There was no other man for the job but me; if it hadn't been for me . . . because to me, I mean me, she has certain obligations to me. Do you want anything else? You'll be served.

SIER TOMAO. Very well, how? When? Where?

RUZANTE. [*getting ready to speak*] Listen, master. When I was a boy, after I stopped playing with animals, when I had that dog I told you about, who followed by my hand, I began going with girls, because my heart wasn't in it with livestock. I began going to parties every night, sometimes three and four miles away in darkness deep as a wolf's mouth.

SIER TOMAO. What the devil does this have to do with me? What has the moon got to do with shrimps? I ask you how we are faring in this matter of mine, and you talk about your cattle driving, your partying, your pooping!

RUZANTE. Cattle, right to the point. Listen, please; quiet, please; this is right to the point. Hear me, if you will. [*He begins again*]. And so, as I was about to say, about going to parties, sometimes I went more than eight miles. Yes indeed! To me it was a piece of cake, or a doughnut . . . and then, as I was about to say, one night didn't I meet a wolf, his two eyes glowing like candles, as tall as a big ass?

SIER TOMAO. [*twitching*] Twat, you'll make me knock down Saint Mark . . . What the devil do wolves have to do with my affair? I want to talk about love and you tell me about people-eating wolves.

RUZANTE. I want to speak of love too, and of your love. Hear me, if you will.

SIER TOMAO. Concerning me? Regarding me?

RUZANTE. Concerning you, in your respect.

SIER TOMAO. [*rassegnato*] Orsú, va' drio, mo compie 48
piú presto che ti puol.

RUZANTE. E sí, con a' ve dego rivar de dire de sto lovo, 49
a' cato sto lovo: e sto lovo me guardava mi, e mi el guardava elo, e elo me guardava mi. Ben sa che, per farghe
paura, a' fazo: «Bruuu, bruuu, buu!...». [*Si avventa su Sier
Tomao facendo l'urlo del lupo*].

SIER TOMAO. [*colto alla sprovvista, si spaventa davvero*] Te 50
vegna el cagasangue, ti e i to lovi! Ti me ha fato scampar
quanto sangue avea adosso. No te usar a farme de sti spà-
semi e de sti ati da bestia.

RUZANTE. [*si finge mortificato*] Mo a' he fato per far con 51
a' fi'. [*Riattacca*] E sí, con a' ve dego rivar de dire, el no
vosse aver paura, sto lovo, a' 'l laghiè stare. Aéa un spon-
ton, a' me 'l strapegava drio, e sí a' me fiè ben pí de cento
crose, con le man, con la lengua, a' dissi el triàbiti,² la
salveregina...

E sí, con a' ve dego rivar de dire, andasea a filò. Bessà 52
che de fato tuti saea che a' iera cantarin. A' se metívinu
a cantare, a zugare a purassé zuoghi: al beco mal guardò,
a la passarela, e, con avívinu zugò, a' se metèvino a far
ravolò; e man per tuto el fogolaro nomé çielo e gusse de
ravi. E ela dasea da bevere a tuti, e mi a' bevea; e ela dasea
tal fià sonda, e mi in tolea; e sí a' magnava, e ela se la
risea, e mi me la risea, ela me çignava, e mi a' ghe çignava
a ela; le me guardava mi, e mi a' la guardava ela.

SIER TOMAO. No te digo che ti no faveli a preposito? 53
Ti parli del fato to de ti, e mi vogio saver del fato mio
de mi.

RUZANTE. Pota, mo a' si' insorío! Mo laghème dire, 54
che a' vegnirè col me in lo vostro.

SIER TOMAO. [*smaniando*] Non puol far, mi e chi me ha 55
inzenerao, che sta cossa sia al mio preposito. E' ho pur
bon natural, no ghe cato zà né cao né via che la possa
vegnir a mio proposito.

SIER TOMAO. [*resigned*] Onward, go ahead, but get there as fast as you can.

RUZANTE. Yes, as I was saying about this wolf, I met this wolf; and the wolf stared at me, and I stared at him, and he stared at me. Well, to frighten him I went: "Broo, boo!" [*He lunges at Sier Tomao, howling like a wolf*].

SIER TOMAO. [*taken by surprise, he is genuinely frightened*] Bloody shit on you, you and your wolves! You've made my blood vessels burst. Don't get in the habit of giving me frights with these wild-animal acts.

RUZANTE. [*pretending to be mortified*] But I did it to show you how I behaved. [*He begins again*]. Yes, as I was about to say, he wouldn't take fright, that wolf, so I let him be. I had a lance that I carried with me, and I made more than a hundred crosses, with my hand; with my tongue, I said the *Qui habitat,* the *Salve regina . . .*

Yes, as I was about to say, I was going to a party. Bessa and everyone else knew I was a singer. We began singing and playing games: the badly watched billy goat, the lady passing by; and after we finished playing we set to eating turnips, and around the whole fireside there was nothing beneath the sky but turnip peels. She gave everyone something to drink, and I drank, and she passed around some [turnip] slices and I helped myself; and while I was eating she laughed, and I laughed; she made me a sign, and I made her a sign; she looked at me, and I looked at her.

SIER TOMAO. Didn't I tell you that you are not speaking to the point? You are talking about your affair and I want to know about mine.

RUZANTE. Twat, you're impatient! Just let me speak and I'll get from my business to yours.

SIER TOMAO. [*raving*] It cannot be, by the person who begat me, that this stuff concerns me. I have good sense, but I can see no rhyme or reason as to how this concerns me.

RUZANTE. Mo s'a' ve dighe ch'a' intrerè col me in lo 56
vostro! A' sè an mi che, a no dir pí altro, el no ghe vegnerà. Mo aldí, abiè un puo' de pasinzia.

[*Riattacca*] E sí, con a' ve dego rivar de dire, quando a'
me partía, a' disea cossí pian che a' ghe volea ben a ela; e
ela disea che la m'in volea a mi, e mi disea che iera inamorò in lo fato so de ela, e ela in lo fato me de mi. Con
andasea de festa a messa, a' me petava de fato a la rega,
fra i gi uomeni e le femene; e mi fasea vista de dir pater-
nuostri, e sí disea: «A' ve vò ben a vu, a' son inamorò in
lo fato vostro de vu, a' ve vora' vu». E ela disea che la
fasea cossí an ela.

E po andasea al so cano[lò] a favelar co ela; e avea un 57
cortelo che rasava, a' tolea un canuolo, e sí fasea cossí d'i
suoldi, o con un'asta a' segnava in tera, e sí a' favelava co
ela. L'aéa mo una bambasina bianca, che la parea un pa-
veio. E mi disea: «A' si' pur bela, a' me piasí pure». E ela
diea: «A' si' belo an vu, a' me parí un pomo museto». E
mi diea: «A' me parí un pomo çielà, bianco e rosso co' è
un velú de sea». E ela diea: «Mo vu, ch'a' sonè un calan-
drato, a cantare?» E mi a' diea: «E vu, che parí un guin-
dolo, a balare?» A' no me volea lagar batere de parole.

SIER TOMAO. Mo compie ancúo, per l'amor de Dio! 58
Hastu compío? O èstu a la mitae?

RUZANTE. Missier sí, adesso a' riverè; aldí pure, tasí 59
pure. [*Riattacca*] E sí, con a' ve dego rivar de dire, anda-
sívinu a le feste, e mi andasea da i pivi,[3] e sí ordenava un
balo. A' no volea mé altro ca pavana:[4] e man a' tolea su
sta puta, e po man a balare, d'agnora con sto pè maístro
inanzo! E man sta puta se dindolava, che l'ara' balò su 'n
dinaro; e mi a' fasea pieripuoli, e presore cossí [*eseguisce
delle giravolte*], che a' dissè che aesse imparò per ponto de
reson.

SIER TOMAO. Ti compirà pur, co' ti averà balao? Che 60

RUZANTE. I'm telling you, I'll get to you! I also know that if I say no more we'll get nowhere. So listen; be a little patient.

[*He begins again*]. Yes, as I was about to say, as I was leaving I told her quietly that I liked her, and she said she liked me, and I told her that I had fallen in love with her, and she with me. When I went to Mass on holidays I stayed near the doorway, between the men and the women, and I pretended to be saying Our Fathers, but I was really saying, "I love you, I love everything about you, I want you." And she was doing the same.

Then I went over to her pew to speak with her. I had a whittling knife, and I took a cane and shaved chips like coins, and marked the ground with a pole; that's how I spoke to her. She wore a white cotton frock that made her look like a butterfly. And I said: "You're so beautiful, I really like you." And she said: "You're handsome too, like a ripe apple." And I said: "You're like a bright apple, white and red like silken velvet." And she said: "Can you sing like a lark?" And I said to her: "Can you turn like a spinning wheel when you dance?" (I didn't want her to have the last word).

SIER TOMAO. Finish up, for the love of God! Have you finished? Or are you in the middle?

RUZANTE. Yes, master, now I will finish; listen please, quiet please. [*He begins again*]. Yes, as I was about to say, we went to holiday feasts, and I'd go over to the pipers and ask for a dance. I never wanted anything but the Pavane; and I'd catch this girl up and then dance, always with this right foot forward! And the girl whirled around; she'd have danced on a coin. And I made pirouettes and turned like this [*he executes a turn*] so you'd say I had learned for point of honor.

SIER TOMAO. Will you please finish; what happened after you danced? What the devil advice are you giving

diavolo de colegi me dastu? E sí vuol che sta cossa vegna in mio proposito! No védestu che ti disi de ti?

RUZANTE. Mo se a' ve dighe che vegnerè col me in lo vostro? Aldí pure.

SIER TOMAO. Ben: ti balavi, ti saltavi.

RUZANTE. Ma sí! A' no saltava, ché a' no iera massa 61 saltarin. A' balava: chi v'ha dito ch'a' saltava? Mé sí...

SIER TOMAO. Ti balavi. Orsú, e può?

RUZANTE. A' balava per çerto; el no iera gnian lomé 62 un che me avançesse, e sí a' ve dirè an chi. Saívu la Vostra Rebelinzia, cognossissi mé questú? Oh, aièmelo a dire!... Cancaro el magne, che andasea balanto su quante feste iera in Pavana... Quel saltarin...

SIER TOMAO. Sí che 'l cognosso. Che importa questo? 63

RUZANTE. Mo chi ièrolo? Co' aèvelo lome? 64

SIER TOMAO. [seccato] Diavolo, e' me son andao a intri- 65 gar da mia posta. E' no te voio pí responder. [Gli volge le spalle].

RUZANTE. A' di' ch'a' 'l cognossí, e sí no saí gnan [con 66 l'aéa lome]. L'iera quelú che so frelo menà via quela puta de quela massaria, che i vene in costion, che i fè po lite... Che la puta ghe aéa impromentú, e so mare no volea, la puta muzà, so frelo e so serore e elo, so frelo, ghe dè a igi, perché elo no ghe la volea dare... El ghe menè de ramazon, cossí... [Fa l'atto di chi picchia] A' no cognossí gnian altri?

SIER TOMAO. Mo compi. 67

RUZANTE. A' he compío adesso. Laghème dir lomè 68 questo. [Riattacca] E sí, con a' ve dego rivar de dire, de balare la iera mo una putata compía, che no ghe mancava gnente. A' ghe strenzea la man: «O man, maneta da impastar tre furni de pan al dí, man da bragagnar mescole, da menar polenta, peverà e faveta!»⁵ E man a' la lagava, e trasea un saltarelo o na capriola, che andasea in lo àiere.

me? Is this leading to my business? Don't you see that you're talking about yourself?

RUZANTE. Didn't I say that I'll get to you? Listen, please.

SIER TOMAO. Very well: you were dancing, you were jumping.

RUZANTE. Indeed! I did not jump, I wasn't a jumper. I danced: who told you I was jumping? Indeed . . .

SIER TOMAO. You were dancing. Very well, and then?

RUZANTE. I was dancing, to be sure: there was only one man who surpassed me, and I'll tell you who he was. Do you know him, Your Repellence, have you ever met him? Oh, help me remember his name! . . . Canker eat him, he used to go dancing on all the holidays in the Pavano . . . That jumper . . .

SIER TOMAO. Yes I know him. What difference does it make?

RUZANTE. But who was he? What was his name?

SIER TOMAO. [exasperated] The devil, I got myself into this. I'm not answering you any more. [He shrugs his shoulders].

RUZANTE. You say you know him, but you don't know his name. He was the fellow whose brother abducted that girl from the farm, and it became a dispute ending in a brawl . . . because the girl had given him her promise, but her mother was not willing, so the girl ran away, and her brother and sister and he, the brother, came to blows because he wouldn't give her up . . . They went at him with clubs, like this. [He makes a gesture of beating someone]. Don't you at least know the others?

SIER TOMAO. Finish.

RUZANTE. I'm finishing now. Let me just say this. [He begins again]. Yes, as I was about to say, as a dancer she had everything; she lacked nothing. I used to squeeze her hand: "O hand, dear little hand, good for kneading three ovens of bread a day, good for brandishing mixing

127

E po, con aéa rivò de balare, a' me andasea a imbusare   69
drio a qualche çisoto. Pensève con a' fasea, a' me andasea
remenanto, pensantome de ela e de quela man che a'
gh'aéa tocò, che assè dito: «Costú è inorcò». A' stravol-
zeva gi uoci, da tanta smagna che aéa.

SIER TOMAO. [*scoppiando*] Al corpo che no digo, ti me   70
fa vegnir ambastia e stravolzer i oci anche mi, e me vien
i suori de la morte! Avesse almanco dove sentar; el me
besogna star ascoltar sti to imbertoneçi al mio despeto,
varda se 'l diavolo fa ben.

RUZANTE. Mo a' taserè, se a' no volí ch'a' dighe. Che   71
me fa a mi? El dee esser fuossi per mi, questo? A' ve
dighe per vegnir a dir de vu, mi.

SIER TOMAO. Va' drio, per to fe', mo compie presto.

RUZANTE. [*riattacca*] E sí, co' a' ve dego rivar de dire,   72
una festa... [*Si interrompe*] A' no me recordo ben che festa
foesse, da San Lorenzo, o da San Piero... A' falo, el fo
una domenega, o un sabo che iera festa, che magniè scar-
dole su la graela, che no me 'l desmentegherè mé... O fo
pur un zuobia?

SIER TOMAO. Sia che zorno se voia: un zorno de festa,   73
una volta; compie.

RUZANTE. Missier sí, missier sí. A' la meniè da un fes-   74
taro, e sí a' gh'impi' el grembiale de braçiè, de nubiè,
de fugaçine, de braçiè fuorti, ch'a' spisi bonamen pí de
çinque marchiti.

SIER TOMAO. Ben, buzolai. Ti ghe in comprassi, e può?   75

RUZANTE. E po, con a' ve dego rivar de dire, a' la com-   76
pagniè a ca', ch'i stasea su una possi[ssi]on de un me
amigo, che iera cossí un çerto poltronazo, con a' fossè
mo vu, che a' fossè me amigo, intendíu? E po, con a'
fússino a ca': «Stè la bona sera, andè la bona sera...»

spoons to stir polenta, peppers, and beans!" Then I'd let her hand go and take a leap or a cartwheel high up in the air.

Then when I finished dancing, I stepped behind some bush. You can imagine what I did, I was so agitated thinking about that hand I had touched, you'd have said: "That man is bewitched." My eyes would bulge from the frenzy I was in.

SIER TOMAO. [*exploding*] By whose body I won't say, you're making me breathe hard and my eyes bulge, and I'm in a deathly sweat! If I at least had some place to sit down; I have to stay and listen to your foolishness in spite of myself; see if it docs any the devil good.

RUZANTE. Then I'll be silent if you don't want me to speak. What does it matter to me? Am I doing this for myself? I am talking so I can get to you.

SIER TOMAO. Go ahead, by your faith, but finish quickly.

RUZANTE. [*he begins again*] Yes, as I was about to say, one holiday . . . [*He interrupts himself*]. I don't remember exactly which holiday it was, the feast of Saint Lawrence or of Saint Peter . . . I'm wrong, it was a Sunday, or a Saturday that fell on a feast day, because I ate grilled rudds I'll never forget . . . or was it a Thursday?

SIER TOMAO. Let it be any day you want: a feast day, once upon a time; finish.

RUZANTE. Yes, master, yes master. I took her to a baker and filled her apron with biscuits and wafers and buns and doughnuts; I spent well over five marks.

SIER TOMAO. Very well, doughnuts. You bought them for her, and then?

RUZANTE. And then, as I was about to say, I accompanied her to her home, which was on the property of a friend of mine, a mean coward, as you would be if you weren't my friend, you understand? Then when we got to the house: "Good evening, have a good evening . . ."

SIER TOMAO. Bona sera, bon ano.[6] Ti ha compío? Ben,   77
a che sèla al mio proposito del mio amor?

RUZANTE. No, aldí. El vene po le guere, con a' saí, che   78
tuti muzava; e mi a' fu' pigiò. Cancaro, el me pigiè no
so che Toíschi, che i me scapè squaso le ongie! I favelava
in toesco, cancaro i magne! Sta puta muzè per le muzaruole, e mi e ela a' no se avívino miga imprometú ancora. La muzè per le muzaruole. A' no l'he mé pí vezúa,
ela, missier no.

SIER TOMAO. Ben, hastu compío?

RUZANTE. Mo a' he compío. Mo a' no v'he gnian dito,   79
quando i Toíschi me pigiè, a comuò i fè. Cancaro, l'è na
filatuoria lunga! Mo a' he compío de questo, missier sí.

SIER TOMAO. Mo che diavolo de mio proposito sè   80
questo? Ela, ela, ela: chi sè sta ela? E' vorave pur saver se
l'è madona Doraliçe.

RUZANTE. No, cancaro! L'è la puta che sta con ela. La   81
se ha recordò adesso d'i braçiè, e sí ha favelò pre vu a
madona Raliçe.

SIER TOMAO. Va', diavolo, va', adesso intendo! Ti me   82
'l podevi dir in do parole, e sí ti me ha tegnúo tre ore. Ti
me vol dir che per i buzolai che ti ghe comprassi, la te
[ha] fato sto servissio, che l'ha parlao per mi a madona
Doraliçe. Ti 'l podevi pur dir in do parole.

RUZANTE. Mo sí, i de' esser çelegati da cavar fuora   83
d'una busa in do branchè.

SIER TOMAO. Ben, che ordene hastu messo con ela,   84
tandem?[7]

RUZANTE. [*candido*] Mo a' n'he metú ordene negun.   85

SIER TOMAO. Va', pota de Santa Cataruza,[8] semo intro   86
i primi termeni! [*Gridando*] Con chi songio intrigao, in
che muodo sarògio mo servío? On' sè sta bona novela
che ti disevi?

SIER TOMAO. Good evening, good-bye. Have you finished? What does this have to do with the business of my love?

RUZANTE. Well, listen. Then came the wars, as you know, when everyone fled and I was taken prisoner. Blast, I was captured by some Germans, who nearly pulled out my nails! They spoke German, pox eat them! The girl fled with the refugees, and she and I weren't yet betrothed. She left with the refugee families. And I never saw her again, no sir.

SIER TOMAO. Well, have you finished?

RUZANTE. I've finished. But I haven't told you anything about what the Germans did when they captured me. Blast, that's a long tale! I have finished this part, yes master.

SIER TOMAO. What the devil does this have to do with me? The girl, the girl, the girl: who is this girl? I'd like to know if it's Madam Doralice?

RUZANTE. No, blast it! It's the girl she has with her. She still remembers the doughnuts, and she has spoken to Madam Spicy about you.

SIER TOMAO. Go on, the devil, go on, now I understand! You could have told me in two words and you've kept me for three hours. You mean to tell me that for the doughnuts that you bought her she's done you the service of speaking to Madam Doralice on my behalf. You could have said so in two words.

RUZANTE. Yes, if they'd been fledgling sparrows to dig out of a hole in two handfuls.

SIER TOMAO. Well, what arrangement have you made with her, pray tell?

RUZANTE. [candidly] I haven't made any arrangement.

SIER TOMAO. Go on, Saint Pussy-Kate, we're back to the very beginning! [Shouting] Who am I dealing with? How am I being served? What is this good news you were talking about?

131

RUZANTE. [*offeso*] A' no arè gnian fato niente, chi 87
v'alde. N'hegi fato assé, che la no cre' ch'a' sipiè pí cossí
burto omo, con iera stò dito, e che vu a' ghe falerí?

SIER TOMAO. Donca ti no ha parlao con essa? 88

RUZANTE. Va', cancaro, va'! No ve dighe che a' he fa- 89
velò co la mia pre vu? Le se favelerà mo una co l'altra, e
po vu a' ghe andarí a favelare. Mo el besogna che a' no
ve perdè, co' a' ghe falerí, ch'a' ghe sapiè dire el fato
vostro, che a' ghe volí ben, e che a' si' inamorò in ela, e
che da biè mé ela; e che, se a' no avessè moiere, a' no
tossè mé altra femena ca ela, e che co' 'l supia morta
vostra moiere, a' la torí ela, e che a' la farí star a muò una
dona, intendíu? E dîghe an de quel'altra, che me vuoia
ben a mi, che da biè mé ele tute do!

SIER TOMAO. Anderòio in casa a parlar con essa, o da i 90
barconi?

RUZANTE. No, cancaro, da i balcon besogna che ghe 91
favelè, perché el no gh'è ordene che andaghè in ca', staganto in sta tera. Mo l'anderà de fuora.

SIER TOMAO. Mo se qualche un d'i soi me vedesse? 92

RUZANTE. A' no sarí miga far vista che 'l fato no supie 93
vostro? Fé vista d'aspetare qualche un. A' no ve sarí miga
pensare qualche noela?

SIER TOMAO. E' digo che i no avesse per mal, che i 94
disesse: «Che fastu qua? Che vol dir sto favelar qua?» E
darme qualche feriaza, intèndestu?

RUZANTE. Pota del cancaro, a' si' spauroso! Assè fato 95
mal, co' a' fasea mi, a' sassè andò de note, co' a' fasea
mi... In lo culo! Che criu che supie paura? La paura no è
altro che imaginarse, pensarse. Fé cossí, aldí. A' vuoio

RUZANTE. [*offended*] One might think I had done nothing, to hear you. Haven't I done enough if she no longer thinks you are the ugly man she had been told, and if I asked if you can speak to her?

SIER TOMAO. Then you didn't speak to her?

RUZANTE. Go on, blast, go on! Didn't I tell you that I spoke with my girl on your behalf? They'll talk to one another, and then you'll go talk to her. But you mustn't get confused when you speak to her; you have to know how to state your business, say that you like her, that you're in love with her, and how fortunate she is; and that if you didn't have a wife, you would take no other woman but her, and that when your wife dies, you'll take her and let her live like a lady, do you understand? And say something about the other girl too, the one who likes me; say they'll both be taken care of!

SIER TOMAO. Shall I speak with her inside her house, or will she be on the balcony?

RUZANTE. No, pox, you'll have to speak to her from the balcony because there's no way for you to get into her house so long as she's in the city. But she's going away.

SIER TOMAO. What if one of her kinfolk should see me?

RUZANTE. Can't you make it appear as if it's no business of yours? Make it look as if you're waiting for someone. Can't you make up some story?

SIER TOMAO. I mean, I don't want them to take it the wrong way, I don't want them to say: "What are you doing here? What is this discussion about?" and do me some harm. Do you understand?

RUZANTE. Blasted twat, you're so fearful! If you'd been as bad as I have, if you'd gone out at night, like me . . . Shove it! What do you think fear is? Fear is nothing but imagining it, thinking about it. Do this, listen. Here is what I want you to do: I'll go in the house and you,

133

che façè a sto muò: mi andarè in ca', e vu in sto mezo
andè drio a sta viazuola, e tornè, che 'l para che 'l fato no
supie vostro, intendíu? Mi a' sarè sul balcon co ela: se a'
me sentí cantare, guardè in su e faveleghe, se a' no me
sentí cantare, andè via de lungo. Moa, andè.

SIER TOMAO. Co' ti canti, che varda in suso?   96

RUZANTE. Missier sí, perché, co' a' cante, no ghe sarà   97
prígolo. Moa, andè. El besogna esser anemusi, a la fe',
chi se vuò inamorare. A' son pur bon da sto mestiero, a'
non ara' paura de Rolando,[9] co' a' son inamorò. [*Bussa
alla porta di Doralice, e chiama*] Olà, olà, o da la ca'! A'
vegnirè entro, mi. Olà! [*Entra in casa*].

SCENA QUARTA

GINEVRA e ISOTTA

GINEVRA. Io non ho desiderato cossa al mondo altra   98
tanto come ritrovarti, dolcissima sorella. E perché vòi
che ora non ti compiacia? Io voglio che tu mi sie sorella,
padre, madre, maestro e baila. Quello che ti è in piacere,
dillo pur sicuramente, che né piú né meno farò.

ISOTTA. Odi, carissima sorella. Tu se' vedoa, e io senza   99
marito; e consumando la nostra giovenezza senza marito,
daremo materia ad ognuno di dire che siamo men che
oneste; senza che grandissimo despiacer ne fia quando
saremo divenute vechie, che staremo a dir le favole con
la gata acanto al focolare. Io voglio che si maritiamo; e
perciò che questo è un nodo perpetuo, devemo con ogni
diligenzia cercare di pigliare uomeni confacevoli a li costumi nostri.

Io son, come a lo albergo ti dissi, tre anni stata schiava   100
insiemme con quelli dui giovani, Tancredi e Teodoro. E

meanwhile, go down this alleyway and turn back so it appears as if you had no business there, do you understand? I'll be on the balcony with her; if you hear me singing, look up and speak to her, but if you don't hear me sing, be off in a flash. Go on.

SIER TOMAO. If you're singing, then I look up?

RUZANTE. Yes, master, if I am singing there will be no danger. Go on. Faith, a man must be brave if he wants to be a lover. I'm really good at this trade; I'm not afraid of Orlando when I'm in love. [*He knocks at Doralice's door, and calls*]. Ola, ola, whoever is home! I'm coming in. Ola! [*He enters the house*].

SCENE FOUR

GINEVRA and ISOTTA

GINEVRA. I have not wanted anything in the world so much as to find you again, sweetest sister. What makes you think I am not happy with you now? I want you to be my sister, father, mother, teacher, and nurse. Speak your pleasure confident that I will do neither more nor less.

ISOTTA. Hear me, dearest sister. You are a widow and I am without a husband; if we consume our youth unmarried, we will give everyone grounds for saying that we are less than chaste, not to mention our own deep regret when we are old and sit by the hearth with a cat and tell tales. I think we should get married, and as the wedding bond is eternal, we must try with all diligence to find men compatible to our ways.

I, as I told you at the inn, was a slave for three years together with those two young men, Tancredi and Teodoro. Without ever revealing to either one of them that I am a woman, I observed their habits very well, and I

ancora che a niuno di loro per donna mi sia manifestata, io ho nottato cossí ben li costumi suoi, che mi pare esser certa che sariano degni di aver per moglie ogni gran donna. E di Tancredi sono stata ferventemente inamorata. Oltre di ciò, sono sciciliani, e richissimi; però mi pareva a me, quando paresse a te, che io dovessi devenir moglie di Tancredi, e tu di Teodoro, e tutti quatro senza indugia ritornarsi ne la patria nostra, a godersi il nostro.

GINEVRA. Io son disposta a compiacerti, fa' tu.

ISOTTA. Cerchiamoli adunque, che, se non averan tro- 101 vato chi li abia riscossi, li riscoterem noi. E ora ora a la volta di Vinegia imbarcati se ne anderemo. E ora che le nostre miserie hanno avuto fine, non piú in questi panni, ma in abito feminile revestite, insiemme con gli sposi nostri nella patria nostra tornaremo. Vogliamo cossí?

GINEVRA. Non te ho detto, sorella mia, che facia tu?   102
[*Partono*].

SCENA QUINTA

RUZANTE, SIER TOMAO e DORALICE

RUZANTE. [*sul balcone di Doralice, canta*]

«E caro amore,   103
e dolce amore,
doname una balestrina...»

SIER TOMAO. [*saluta Doralice*] Dio ve contente, perla 104
mia, zogielo caro.

DORALICE. [*facendosi essa pure al balcone*] Ben vegni
Vostra Signoria, signor mio.

SIER TOMAO. Orben, a che semo nu, an?   105

DORALICE. La vostra cortesia mi ha vinta in modo, che
non posso esser se non vostra, signor mio caro.

am certain that they are worthy to have any grande dame for wife. I myself am fervently in love with Tancredi. Besides, they are Sicilians, and very rich; therefore it seems to me, if you agree, that I should be Tancredi's wife and you Teodoro's, and all four of us shall return to our homeland without delay to enjoy what is ours.

GINEVRA. I am inclined to agree with you; do as you like.

ISOTTA. Then let us look for them so if they haven't found someone to ransom them, we will ransom them ourselves and embark straightaway toward Venice. And now that our sorrows are at an end, no longer in these clothes but dressed again in womanly apparel we shall return with our husbands to our native land. Shall we do so?

GINEVRA. Haven't I told you, my sister, as you like it! [*They leave*].

SCENE FIVE

RUZANTE, SIER TOMAO, and DORALICE

RUZANTE. [*on Doralice's balcony, singing*]

Dear love,
sweet love,
give me a little crossbow . . .

SIER TOMAO. [*he greets Doralice*] God rest you, my pearl, precious jewel.

DORALICE. [*from her balcony*] Well met, Your Lordship, my dear *signore*.

SIER TOMAO. Very well, then, how far are we?

DORALICE. Your courtesy has conquered me so that I can be no one's save yours, my dear *signore*.

137

SIER TOMAO. Vu trazè balote, an? Avè torto.   106

DORALICE. Io naqui a sdigno di fortuna, perché le mie 107
parole non possono esser credute. Io son pur vostra,
quando vi piacia ch'io sia; ben che la moglie vostra me
abia fatto minaciare, io non mi rimarò però di amarvi.

SIER TOMAO. Quel diavolo de mia moier, al sagra- 108
mento mio, ghe voio dar diese bastonae per ste parole. E
perzò, fia bela, fia zentilesca, le nostre cosse fèmole se-
cretamente. Non ston ben qua su la via, che la zente me
veda int'el passar.

DORALICE. Io vi farei entrar in casa, ma queste vicine 109
mie son troppo maledete. Ci sono di quelle che mi fanno
la guardia fino a mezanotte, sol per aver che dire di me:
«La tal fa cossí, la tal fa colà...»

SIER TOMAO. O diavolo! Mala cossa la cativa vesinanza. 110

DORALICE. Io son disposta a compiacervi, ma in questa 111
terra non li è ordine alcuno; e se io non rimanesse per
un poco de impacio, adesso adesso me ne anderia in
villa, e voi ne venireste, e questa sera saressemo insiemme. Ma rimango per uno certo intrico.

RUZANTE. [all'improvviso] Iz, iz, olà, olà! Missier, mis- 112
sier, fé vista.

SIER TOMAO. [disorientato] An? Che sè?   113

RUZANTE. El n'è gnente, cancaro, l'è stò le buele che 114
me bogia. A' crêa che 'l foesse un. Moa, andè drio.

SIER TOMAO. Va', diavolo! Buta i oci de qua e de là. 115

RUZANTE. Butè le regie lunzi, s'a' sentissè qualcossa. 116
Aldí, co' a' subi una bota, to[e]ve via de fato.

SIER TOMAO. [volgendosi di nuovo a Doralice] An, ben 117
mio? An, fia bela? Che disèvu che volè andar in vila?

SIER TOMAO. You're teasing, aren't you? You do me wrong.

DORALICE. Fortune slighted me at birth if my words cannot be believed. I am really yours, if it so please you; even though that wife of yours has threatened me, even so, I cannot help loving you.

SIER TOMAO. That devil of a wife; upon my oath, I'd like to give her ten blows for those words. Therefore, fair child, gentle child, let us keep our matter secret. I should not be here on the street where people may see me as they pass by.

DORALICE. I would have you come into the house, but these neighbors of mine speak too wickedly. There are some women who keep watch on me until midnight just so they can say: "She does this, she does that . . ."

SIER TOMAO. Oh the devil! A wicked neighbor is a curse.

DORALICE. I am prepared to satisfy you, but in this city there is no way; and if I were not staying here on account of a slight entanglement, I would already be on my way to a villa in the country, and you would come, and we would spend this evening together. But I am delayed because of a certain complication.

RUZANTE. [*suddenly*] Iz, iz, ola, ola! Master, master, pretend.

SIER TOMAO. [*confused*] Well? What is it?

RUZANTE. It's nothing, blast it; my stomach was growling. I thought someone was there. Go on, continue.

SIER TOMAO. Go on, the devil! Keep turning your eyes in every direction.

RUZANTE. Perk up your long ears, you may hear something. Listen, if I whistle, leave at once.

SIER TOMAO. [*turning again to Doralice*] Well, my goodness? Well, my lovely child? You were saying that you wanted to go to a house in the country? That you wish

Magari che vu no avessè visinanza che ve desse fastidio. E perché restèvu?

DORALICE. Per un certo impacio, che da Ruzante 118 intendereti.

SIER TOMAO. Ruzante sa, esso? Basta, pur che se possa, 119 al santa sacre de vagnele, non mancarò mai, per far mentir per la gola sti lari, che dise ste zanze de mi, che i meriterave de un pugnal int'i peti.

DORALICE. Non è pegior cossa che la mala lingua.

SIER TOMAO. [*galante e lascivo*] Mo la vostra, zogielo 120 caro, tresoro mio, no sè trista, essa. E' credo che la sia pí dolce che coronela de zucaro. Fia, ben, zugheremoi po, con siemo in vila, an, carne mie?

DORALICE. Io non imparai mai a iocare.   121

SIER TOMAO. No, an? Fina le mamole sa ziogar a sti 122 zioghi che digo mi.

DORALICE. Come se chiamano questi giochi?   123

SIER TOMAO. A le pançe, a la scondaruola... Mi scon- 124 derò, e vu tegnirè ocio.

RUZANTE. [*fischia*] Sbio, iz, iz, sbio, toiónse via! No sè 125 tri o quatro che ven da cao de sta viazuola?

SIER TOMAO. Mogia, a' me recomando, fia bela...:   126 [*Doralice si ritira in fretta*].

RUZANTE. La no gh'è [pí], cancaro, che l'ha abú paura. 127 Cancaro, no vuogio dir, ve vegna! S'a' vuogio, missiere, a' no si' de qui da Figaruolo, de qui buoni. A' sè che gh'aí dito el fato vostro. Cope, Fiorin![1] al sangue, a' no me l'ara' mé pensò. Po i dise, po...

SIER TOMAO. Co', co', cossí?   128

RUZANTE. Co', co'? A' dighe, sò, sò, via dal me cor- 129 tivo! A' parí cossí un stizo coverto in lo viso, e sí a' si' un mal sbregon, vu. A' no l'ara' mé crezú... I provierbii no

there were no neighbors to annoy you. And why are you staying here?

DORALICE. Because of a certain complication that Ruzante will explain.

SIER TOMAO. Ruzante knows, does he? Enough. So long as I am able, by the holy memory of the Evangelists, I'll not fail to show they lie in their throats, those thieves who spread rumors about me, who deserve to have a knife plunged into their hearts.

DORALICE. There's nothing worse than a wicked tongue.

SIER TOMAO. [*gallant and suggestive*] But your tongue, my jewel, my treasure, isn't wicked. It's sweeter than a little sugar crescent. So be it, fine; we'll play sweet games when we go to this villa, won't we, my flesh?

DORALICE. I never learned to play games.

SIER TOMAO. No? Even little ladies know how to play the games I mean.

DORALICE. What are these games called?

SIER TOMAO. Belly roll, hide-and-seek . . . I'll hide and you'll close your eyes.

RUZANTE. [*whistles*] Whew, iz, iz, whew, let's be off! I think there are three or four people coming up the street.

SIER TOMAO. Don't forget, fair child . . .

[*Doralice withdraws hastily*].

RUZANTE. They're gone, pox, what a scare. Canker eat . . . I won't say what! You're no warbler, you get to the point. You told her your intentions. Goblets, for a florin! By the blood, I wouldn't have thought it. And they say. . . .

SIER TOMAO. Say, say, say what?

RUZANTE. Say, say? I say hey, hey, get out of my court! You're a smouldering ember to look at, but you're a wolf in sheep's clothing. I wouldn't have believed it . . . Prov-

falè mé: «Gata piata, fievera ve bata». Cancaro, te pàrsele brombe?

SIER TOMAO. Al sagramento mio, no intendo zò che ti 130 vuol dir de brombole.

RUZANTE. [*sarcastico*] Oh, el no me intende, l'omo, sí 131 e' l'è figo! Mostreve da bona vila. A' sè che a' le saí far inamorar, mi, le pute.

SIER TOMAO. Varda, Ruzante, al corpo de Santa Cata- 132 ruza! La no sè stà mai imbertonà in mi, nomé adesso, e sastu a che muodo?

RUZANTE. Mo sí, mo sí, che a' no 'l sè inanzo che 133 adesso! A' no ve l'he sempre mé dito che la smagna, che la rabia pre vu?

SIER TOMAO. Costie, quando la se acorse che mi iera 134 imbertonà in essa, la se impensà de tegnirme su sti im- bertoneçi, de farme bona çiera, perché no me desberto- nasse, e forsi con anemo pensao de farme trazer. Mo Dio me ha aidao, che la se ha imbertonao essa int'i fati mie, che la non se 'nde ha acorto.

RUZANTE. [*ghignando*] Cossí purpiamen, cossí sparciso. 135 Che ve disèvigi mi? Ve hala dito zò che a' di' fare?

SIER TOMAO. No, la m'ha dito che ti sa ti, e che ti me 136 'l dirà ti.

RUZANTE. La m'ha dito che 'l no gh'è muò che a' possè 137 andar in ca' da ela, staganto ela in sta tera. Mo perché a' ghe possè andare, la vuol andar de fuora, a Arquà.[2]

SIER TOMAO. La me ha dito cossí anche a mi, e che l'ha 138 un çerto intrigo, che la no puol.

RUZANTE. Mo a' ve dirè; la de' dar no sè che dinari, a 139 un, e sti dinari la no gi ha, mo la i de' ben scuore fina un mese. Se la aesse da dàrghegi ancuò, de bel ancuò la an- dera' de fuora, de bel adesso e de bel stasera, po an nu andassàn da ele: da tute do, intendíu?

SIER TOMAO. [*rassegnato*] Ben, dinari. Te hala dito la 140 quantitae?

erbs never lie: "A cat will leap, watch out or weep."
Damn, do you think they're plums?

SIER TOMAO. Upon my oath, I don't know what you
mean by plums.

RUZANTE. [*sarcastic*] Oh, the man doesn't understand
me, he's so simple! You play innocent. I think you know
how to make girls fall in love.

SIER TOMAO. Look here, Ruzante, by the body of
Saint Kate! I've never been loved if I'm not loved now,
and do you know why?

RUZANTE. Of course, of course, didn't I say so before
now? Haven't I always said that she burns, she yearns
for you?

SIER TOMAO. When that woman realized I had fallen
for her, she considered taking advantage of my folly, of
leading me on so I wouldn't lose interest, and perhaps
deep down she thought she'd get something out of me.
But Heaven has come to my aid because she's fallen for
me without knowing how it happened.

RUZANTE. [*grinning*] Just so, exactly so. What did I tell
you? Did she say what you have to do?

SIER TOMAO. No, she said that you know and you'll
tell me.

RUZANTE. She told me that there's no way for you to
get into her house while she remains in the city. So in
order to let you in, she wants to go away, to Arquà.

SIER TOMAO. She told me that too, but because of a
certain complication she cannot leave yet.

RUZANTE. I'll explain; she has to give some money to
someone, but she doesn't have the money now, she'll
have it at the end of the month. If she could make the
payment immediately, then she could leave right away,
this very evening, and we would go with her, both of us,
do you understand?

SIER TOMAO. [*resigned*] Very well, money. Did she say
how much?

RUZANTE. Quanti dinari? Missier sí. Centro lire, de 141
lí via.

SIER TOMAO. Lire de grossi, o de pízoli?[3]   142

RUZANTE. A' cherzo che a' fassè megio darghe smoza- 143
nighe e marçie[gi],[4] ca darghe beze, ché la pora' star
tanto a lumbrare, che a' no andessàn stasera. E mi a' ghe
dissi che la no guardesse a dinari, co' a' me aví dito, e se
no bastava çento, a', ghe 'n darí an un megiaro; e che i
poltron, che ghe ha dito le parole du vu, no fara' miga
cossí, igi.

SIER TOMAO. Ti ha fato ben. Oh, ti sè stà acorto, pota 144
che no digo!

RUZANTE. Ve vàgogi mo per carezà? Che criu che su- 145
pie? A' no dara' la lengua a un altro, per favelare.

SIER TOMAO. Andemo a casa, che te darò i danari, che 146
ti ghe i porterà. Magari andassemo stasera, ghe fosse
ordene.

RUZANTE. Che? L'è ancora grand'ora a sera. Stasera: no 147
me l'hala dito a mi?

RUZANTE. How much money? Yes master. About a hundred lire.

SIER TOMAO. In bills or coin?

RUZANTE. I think it would be better to give her large bills rather than coins, which could take a while to count, so we wouldn't go this evening. I told her you don't care about money, as you said, and that if a hundred weren't enough, you'd give her a thousand; and that the coward who told her stories about you would not do as much.

SIER TOMAO. You did well. Oh, you've been shrewd, you piece of—never mind.

RUZANTE. Have I done well? Who do you think I am? I wouldn't swap my tongue for any other when it comes to storytelling.

SIER TOMAO. Let's go home; I'll give you the money and you take it to her. I hope we find a way to go this very evening.

RUZANTE. Why not? There's still time until evening. This evening: isn't that what she said?

TANCREDI, GINEVRA, TEODORO e ISOTTA

TANCREDI. Deh, perché, dolce Isota, moglie mia, non 1
vi siete manifestata a me nel tempo, che siamo stati
schiavi? Quanti lieti giorni abiam perduto! Le nostre
passioni sariano state men gravi, almanco li primi fruti
d'amore averissimo colti onestamente insiemme. Ma
converà che, radopiando li amorosi abraziamenti, avan-
ziamo quel che per adrieto abiam perduto. E siamo,
come in volgar proverbio si suol dire, quatro corpi e
una sol'anima. Non sarà cossí, madonna Genevra, co-
gnata mia?

GINEVRA. Signor sí; e quanto per me, non pregarò Idio 2
tanto de altra cossa, quanto che il rimanente di nostra
vita sia in modo, che tuti quatro de un medesimo volere
viviamo. Cossí potessimo le noçe celebrare! Ma ne la
patria nostra le celebraremo.

TEODORO. E perché non deverò io pregare continua- 3
mente Idio? Qual compagnia mi potrà esser piú a grado
di questa? E moglie e sorella mi siete, una e l'altra.

ISOTTA. Cossí Idio el viagio nostro prosperi, e lieti ove 4
oggi intendiamo di andare ne conduca; come ch'io desidero, che de una medesima voluntà, de un medesimo
desire viviamo.

TANCREDI. O città gloriosa, che sei stata la fine de le 5
nostre adversità e il principio di tanto nostro bene, il guiderdone che meritaresti non posso, né, se avesse piú poter del poter de tuti gli omeni del mondo insiemme,
potria darte il guiderdone conveniente a tanto dono. Ma
il Sommo Motore ne prego che lo ti renda, come quello
a cui nulla è impossibile. E l'amor, la cortesia, la genti-
lezza, la magnificenzia de' tuoi signori, de' tuoi egregii

ACT FIVE

SCENE ONE

TANCREDI, GINEVRA, TEODORO, and ISOTTA

TANCREDI. Oh why, my sweet wife Isotta, didn't you reveal yourself to me when we were slaves? How many happy days have we lost! Our agonies might have been less severe, and we would have garnered at least love's first fruits virtuously together. But now by doubling our loving embraces let us recover what we lost before. Let us be like the proverb in the vernacular, "four bodies and one soul." Will it not be thus, Madam Ginevra, my sister-in-law?

GINEVRA. Yes, sir; and for my part I shall pray God for nothing more than that for the rest of our lives all four of us may live as one. Would that our nuptials were already celebrated! But let us celebrate them in our homeland.

TEODORO. Shall I not thank God continually? What company could be more welcome to me than this? You are my wife and my sister.

ISOTTA. May God prosper our voyage and conduct us happily to the destination we set out for on this day, for I, too, wish us to live with one and the same will and desires.

TANCREDI. O glorious city, you have seen the end of our adversities and the beginning of our well-being; the reward you merit I cannot give you; not even if I had more power than all the men in the world combined could I give you a reward befitting so great a gift. But I pray that the Highest Mover, to whom nothing is impossible, may render it to you. And may the love, courtesy, nobility, and splendor of your gentlemen, of your distinguished citizens, of your most noble women, al-

citadini, de le tue nobillissime donne sempre in onore
tenga, e te soto tranquila pace governi, e di abundanzia
ti colmi, te difenda contra ogni furore de' tuoi inimici,
ti guardi da ogni loro insidia; e piú presto di ogni tuo
lieto e pacifico stato si dogliano li mali vicini tuoi, che
tu ad alcuno porti invidia. E il nome de li chiari spirti,
che in te albergano, rimanga al monodo con eterna fama.
Città, per mille e mille opre famosa, rimante in pace.
[*Partono*].

SCENA SECONDA

RUZANTE e MENATO, poi BESSA

[*Ruzante e Menato entrano in scena e cantano una matti-
nata sotto la casa di madonna Doralice. Finito il canto, Ruzante dice*]:

RUZANTE. Caro frelo, cantóne un'altra; e nu du can-   6
tó[n]la in quatro. Mi solo a' canterè ben in du: aldi:
[*gorgheggia*]

«E de la mala morte»...

Vitu, co' 'l grosso tase, el sotil canta, e co' 'l sotil tase, el
grosso canta.

MENATO. Al sangue del cancaro, l'è ben bela, chi   7
poesse fare an che una vaca tiresse per do, e du pan fesse
per quatro.

RUZANTE. Per magnare, a' magnera' ben per du, e per   8
cantare. Mo per laorare, a' laoro lomé per mezo un.
Moa, scomenza.

MENATO. A' te dighe ch'a' he priessia, che a' he Me-   9
nego Trelesato che me aspieta. A' irò fuora de la porta.
Làgheme anare; t'he bon cantare, zà che la te va da
canto.

RUZANTE. Di' lomé questa, una bota, caro frelo.   10

ways honor you and govern you in tranquil peace and fill you brimful with abundance, defend you against the violence of your enemies, guard you from every attack, and may your wicked neighbors sooner lament your all-happy and peaceful state than you envy any other. And may the name of the illustrious spirits who reside within you live on in the world in eternal fame. City, famous for thousands and thousands of deeds, live in peace.

[*They leave*].

SCENE TWO

RUZANTE and MENATO, then BESSA

[*Ruzante and Menato enter and sing a song beneath the window of Madam Doralice's window. When the song is fin-ished, Ruzante says*]

RUZANTE. Brother dear, let's sing another, and we two will sing it for four. Alone I sing well for two: listen: [*he sings*]

And of wretched death . . .

You see, when the bass is silent, the top part sings, and when the top part is silent, the bottom part sings.

MENATO. Blasted blood, it would be nice if one cow could pull for two and two loaves serve for four.

RUZANTE. When it comes to eating, I can eat enough for two, and the same for singing. But when it comes to working I work for half of one. Go on, begin. ·

MENATO. I tell you I'm in a hurry. Menego Trelesato is waiting for me. I'm going outside the city gate. Let me go; you sing well because your life is like a song.

RUZANTE. Sing just this one, dear brother.

MENATO. A' dirè per farte cossa a piasere, co' disse   11
quelú. Mo, a la fe', a' he priessia.

RUZANTE. Poh, va' al bordelo! Te sè pur se an mi, con   12
disse quelú...

[*Si accordano e cantano*].

MENATO. Moa, a' vuò mo andare. Portate da per-   13
d'omo. La te buta ben, a ti, e sí te va da canto, che te
magni co' fa i cavagi d'i tiraore, col cao in lo saco.

RUZANTE. Puoh, che vuotu ch'a' faghe? A' stago co sto   14
zentiluomo vegio, e sí a' magno. L'è inamorò, elo, e mi
a' ghe porto i messiti. El no sa che farme, sempre mé:
«Ruzante, magna, magna». E mi a' magno. «Ruzante,
bivi». E mi a' bevo. «Ruzante, merenda, fa' colazion». E
mi a' la fago. Puh sí! E po madona ha tanto piasere del
me cantare, che no besogna dire, Mare Biata!...

MENATO. Mo la de' essere inamorà an ela, n'è vero?   15

RUZANTE. Pensate! Mato el can, mato el buò, mato   16
colú che 'l para. El se favela lomé de amore, in quela ca',
e massare e madona, tuti a scazafasso, fina le banche, i
scagni, le casse sente d'amore. El no gh'è buso, in ca', né
ordegno, che no sapie d'amore.

MENATO. Mo a' no di' star lomé in veragaia tuti, vu.   17

RUZANTE. No favelar de piasere, el no se sente lomé   18
cantar, per quela ca'. Mo laga, s'te saíssi la pí gran noela...
Oh, s'te n'aíssi priessia, a' te fara' pur rire.

MENATO. Te me la dirè po un'altra fià. A' vuò andar,   19
roman ti. [*Esce*].

RUZANTE. Mo va' in susio, s'te vuò ch'a' romagna mi.   20
[*A Bessa, che è apparsa alla finestra*] A' v'he ben vezú zà
un pezato, mo perché el no se n'adesse, no ve guardava.
Aón cantò pre vu, vi'.

BESSA. A' sè che a' la smenuzolè, mi. Vergene Mare   21
Biata, che avíu in quela lengua?

MENATO. I'll sing it for your sake, as they say. But by my faith, I have to hurry.

RUZANTE. Poh, go to the brothel! You know that I'd, . . . as they say.

[*They sing together*].

MENATO. Up now, I have to go. Be an honest man. You live well, you do, like a song, and you eat like a draft horse with his head in the sack.

RUZANTE. Pooh, what do you want me to do? I live with this old gentleman, and I eat. He's in love and I carry the messages. He doesn't know what to do for me; it's always: "Ruzante, eat, eat." And I eat. "Ruzante, drink." And I drink. "Ruzante, have a snack, have a bite." And I do it. Oh yes! And then madame takes more pleasure in my singing than I can say, Blessed Mother! . . .

MENATO. She must be in love too, is she?

RUZANTE. Think of it! Mad the dog, mad the ox, mad the driver. They speak of nothing but love in this house, maids and mistress, all topsy-turvy; the very benches, the seats, the chests smack of love. There's no crevice in the house, nor tool, that doesn't know love.

MENATO. You must all be in heat.

RUZANTE. Say nothing of pleasure; one hears nothing but singing in that house. Wait, if you knew the best tale . . . Oh, if you weren't in a hurry I'd make you laugh.

MENATO. You'll tell me some other time. I have to go; you stay. [*He exits*].

RUZANTE. Well, go to the devil, if you want me to stay behind. [*To Bessa, who has appeared at the window*] I caught sight of you a while ago, but I didn't look up so he wouldn't notice you. I was singing for you.

BESSA. I say, you are a songbird. Blessed Virgin Mother, what do you have on that tongue?

RUZANTE. Ma sí, el no me sa gnian ben aiare. Se aesse   22
chi me aiasse, a' fara' ben de belo. Ve sè dir che 'l no fo
mé zarambela che sonesse miegio de quel che a' fassàn
nu. Vegní, avrí, che a' he i dinari. [*Le fa cenno di scendere
ad aprire e, mentre attende, muove qualche passo di danza*]
To, torindon, dorindon, dorin...
   [*Bessa apre la porta e lo fa entrare*].

SCENA TERZA

SIER TOMAO solo

SIER TOMAO. [*esce di casa*] E' son in gran fastidio, che   23
no me so pensar che scusa catar con sta mia moier, se per
ventura ancúo me convegnerà andar in vila con madona
Doraliçe. *Tamen*[1] el me sbate el cuor; no so co' farà Ruzante, se 'l ghe sarà ordene, sta sera.
   E' voio tornar a casa, per spassar tempo fina che 'l vien   24
Ruzante. Dio el voia che sta bestia de mia moier sia contenta che vada. [*Rientra*].

SCENA QUARTA

RUZANTE solo, poi SIER TOMAO

RUZANTE. [*esce dalla casa di Doralice*] Oh, sea laldò Dio!   25
Andarón pur stasera tuti a Arquà. El vegio no arà magnò
indarno el confeto e i pignuoli arpigiè, né de qui che
ven d'oltra mare, mostachi, morachi, che fa bona forza.
Gnian mi a' n'arè magnò indarno le croste de formaio
salò, né qui tri pan tanto fati, né bevú indarno de quel
vin, che ha una vena de reçento, che Mare Biata!...
   Cancaro, l'è pur la bela putata! L'è lomé late e vin, la   26
de' aver tanto de gamba, tanto de lacheto, tanto de ze-
nuocio, tanto de cossa... Oh, che—pota ch'a' no digo

RUZANTE. Oh, that man doesn't know how to sing with me. If I had someone who could, I'd really be good. I tell you there's never been a piper who sounded better. Come, open up, I have the money. [*He motions for her to come down and open the door, and while he is waiting he does a few dance steps*]. To, torindon, dorindon, dorin . . .

[*Bessa opens the door and lets him come in*].

SCENE THREE

SIER TOMAO alone

SIER TOMAO. [*coming out of the house*] I'm very troubled; I can't think of an excuse to give this wife of mine if luck lets me go to the country today with madam Doralice. Still, my heart is pounding; I don't know what Ruzante can do, whether he can arrange it for this evening.

I'll go back home to pass the time until Ruzante comes. Please God, let this witless wife of mine be glad I am going. [*He goes back in*].

SCENE FOUR

RUZANTE alone, then SIER TOMAO

RUZANTE. [*coming out of Doralice's house*] God be praised! We're really going to Arquà this evening, all of us. The old man won't have eaten sugared almonds and crushed pine nuts for naught, nor those sweets from across the sea—spice cakes, rice cakes—for strength. Nor will I have eaten salty cheese rinds for naught and three good loaves of bread, or drunk for naught that wine with a vein of sparkle, that Blessed Mother . . . !

Damn, she's a handsome girl! She's all milk and wine,

male!—che bel piaser a' se darón in qui buschi. El vegio el sta assé a vegnir. El m'ha pur dito che l'aspiete da chialò via... [*Passeggia, in attesa*].

SIER TOMAO. [*esce ancora di casa*] E' no posso star fermo, 27 e' ho el mal de la formigola. Amor me travaia, el par che aspete una sentenzia de lite... [*Ha un singhiozzo nervoso*] Eh, ehn! El me vien i susti de la morte, e' sento ben mi. Dio el voia che no traza i danari. [*Scorge il servitore, e lo chiama*] Ruzante, Ruzante! E' no te osso domandar... A che semo?

RUZANTE. È la megior noela, la no poea andar miegio. 28 El besogna mo che a' supiè un omo, da chí indrío. Le va via adesso adesso, e sí me ha dito ch'a' dibiamo andar, che da biè mé mi, che 'l gh'è lomé çielo e buschi, che a' n'arón paura almanco che negun ne faza la guarda. On' volívu la pí bela comelitè al mondo? E sí a' se darón piasere de dí e de note. Con volívu i pí biè contenti?

SIER TOMAO. [*torvo*] Fato sta che tuti no sarà contenti, 29 se me parto, Ruzante.

RUZANTE. Mo chi seràgi? 30

SIER TOMAO. Mo madona non serà contenta. 31

RUZANTE. Puoh sí! A' vò ch'a' catè qualche scusa. A' 32 cherzo che la no serà contenta gnian se a' ghe stassè ben a pè, mi.

SIER TOMAO. Per che rason?

RUZANTE. Perché, dasché l'ave quel despeto de quelú 33 che la crêa che 'l foesse un omo, e iera una femena, la sè stà sempre deveosa, de mala vuoia, a muò un dugo a pesso. E perzóntena a' digo che la no serà gnan contenta s'a' ghe stassè ben a pè.

SIER TOMAO. Che diavolo de scusa me poràvio impen- 34 sar? E' me voio consegiar con ti. Se digo de andar a muar àiere, el sè una matieria.

RUZANTE. Mo aponto questa è bona. 35

SIER TOMAO. No, perché e' son vegnúo in sta tera per 36 muar àiere. La dirà: «Onde volèu andar? No sè bon àiere

and she must have such legs, such thighs, such knees, such and such . . . Oh, twat—I won't say it—what a good time we'll have in those bushes. The old man is taking his time getting here, but he said to wait for him in this spot . . . [*He walks around, waiting*].

SIER TOMAO. [*again, coming out of his house*] I can't keep still, I've got ants in my pants. Love torments me as if I were awaiting sentence after a trial . . . [*He sighs nervously*]. Eh, ehem! Let death tremors come over me, I feel fine. Please God I haven't wasted my money. [*He looks for his servant and calls him*]. Ruzante, Ruzante! I daren't ask . . . At what point are we?

RUZANTE. The news couldn't be better. From now on you must be a man. They are going away right now, and they told me we should come too, happy me, where there'll be nothing beneath the sky but woods, where we needn't be afraid of anyone seeing us. Isn't this the best opportunity in the world? We'll take our pleasure day and night. Who could be happier?

SIER TOMAO. [*grim*] The truth is that not everyone will be happy if I leave, Ruzante.

RUZANTE. Who will not?

SIER TOMAO. My lady will not be happy.

RUZANTE. Well yes! You have to make some excuse. But I don't believe she's happy having you underfoot.

SIER TOMAO. Why not?

RUZANTE. Because ever since her vexation over that woman she mistook for a man she's been constantly sulky and bad humored, like an owl on a pole. So I don't think she'd be happy having you underfoot.

SIER TOMAO. What devil of an excuse can I think up? I want your advice. It's foolish to say I am going for a change of air.

RUZANTE. But that's the very thing.

SIER TOMAO. But I came here for a change of air. She'll say: "Where do you want to go? Isn't the air good here?"

155

qua?» E' voio dir che voio andar a veder çerte tere per comprar. Sèla dessa?

RUZANTE. Oh, missier sí, missier sí! Pota, a' ve l'aí 37 pensà bela. Mo andè a ca' presto, e mi a' starè chialò a vêr se in sto mezo le andaesse via; ché a' vuò che andagón in la barca don' le va ele, che a' se smorezeremo co gi uoci almanco. Andè via presto, e asiè le robe che a' volí ch'a' porte, che a' le tornerè a tuore po mi. Mo andè via presto, mo corí presto... [Lo incalza verso casa].

SIER TOMAO. [si rivolta, furioso] Va', diavolo! Vustu che 38 me scavaza el colo? E' voio portar puoche robe: una vesta a la polentina che me meta, son spazao. [Rientra].

RUZANTE. Mo ben, mo ben, andè via presto. [Solo] 39 Guarda che la no se despiere, madona, perché el vaghe via! Fuossi mo che 'l n'è belo da tegnir a pè, el zegio, l'è miegio una fassina de spini assé. Sí, che la n'è inamorà, se mé la no ve' l'ora che 'l se tuoge via? La farà ben vista che 'l ghe recressa, mo la pianzerà co gi uoci e sí se la rirà col cuore.

A' vuò andar a scoltar se i se mete in via, al so usso. [Si 40 accosta all'uscio di Doralice e origlia] Aldi, tasi: a' sento freghezare, a' sento far un gran tampelamento de scagni, de banche, de ciave, de armari. I va da l'altro usso fremamen. Aldi, aldi che la dise: «Passè ben l'usso». Gi è andè via. Cancaro, sto vegio sta assé a vegnir.

O cancaro, arón pur piasere in qui buschi! A' se an- 41 darón imbusanto de drio e denanzo, a' sè ch'a' parerón levraton acalè. Va' via, va' via, a' balerón, el se ghe fa mo festa fin a zenuogio. A' me farè un bel par de calçe s-ciapè, d'i dinari che m'ha dò quela femena d'Ancona, e de qui ch'a' he robò al vegio (che a' n'he dò an a la me puta): un bel par de calçe a la doisa e un bel zuparelo, una bereta rossa con penacio, che ciamerà pute de mile meia. A' son mo ben infornío d'i miè lembri, che 'l no gh'è puta che me vêsse, che no me se apresse. E po a' canto ben, e cossí vestío pur poesse, pur, sopelir a tante!

I'll say I want to go see some properties I'm interested in buying. Will that do?

RUZANTE. Yes, sir, yes, sir! Twat, that's good thinking. Now go home quickly and I'll stay here to keep watch in case they leave in the meantime; I want us to go on the same boat so we can at least embrace with our eyes. Go quickly and prepare the stuff you want to bring, and I'll come back for it. But go quickly, run . . . [*He pushes him toward the house*].

SIER TOMAO. [*turns back, furious*] Go on, go to the devil! Do you want me to break my neck? I'll take just a few things; a coat to relax in and I'm ready. [*He goes back in*].

RUZANTE. Very well, very well, go quickly. [*Alone*] We'll see if milady despairs his going away! Maybe it's better not to keep the lily close by; a bunch of brambles is better. Isn't she in love, too, and can't wait for him to leave? She'll make a show of being sorry, but while her eyes weep her heart will be laughing.

I'll go listen at the door to hear if they're on their way. [*He approaches Doralice's door and puts his ear to it*]. Listen, quiet: I hear a scraping of chairs, of benches, of keys, of chests. They must be going out the other door. Listen, listen, she's saying, "Bolt the door well." They've gone. Damn it, that old man is slow getting here.

Pox, what fun we'll have in those woods. We'll be popping back and forth like hot rabbits. Go on, go on, we'll dance and take a holiday on our legs. I'll get a fine pair of parti-colored hose with the money that I got from that Ancona woman and with what I've taken from the old man (and I gave my girl some too): a fine pair of hose with a stripe and a handsome jacket, a red hat with a plume to beckon girls for a thousand miles. My limbs are so fit that no girl sees me without approaching me. I'm a good singer too, and dressed like that I can satisfy plenty of them! I'll buy a sword; anyone without a good sword dangling out in front doesn't look like a lover.

A' me vuò comprar an una spa', ché chi n'ha una bela spa', che la porte per travesso, no par bon da inamorarse.

Laghème vêr se averè tanti dinari che ghe façe. [*Leva* 42 *di tasca un pugno di monete*] Cancaro, gi è assé! A' no vora' che negun me vêsse. Questo è un ducato d'oro, da Veniesia, venizian; questo un rainese, cavaluoti, moragie, de qui da sie beçe, scarantani[1]... Cancaro, gi è assé dinari! Làgam'i partire: un mucieto è le calçe, l'altro mucieto el zuparelo, st'altro è la bereta. Mo la pena? Tuò un puoco per un d'i muciti... O la spa'? Un puoco del mucio de le calçe, del mucio del zuparelo, del mucio de la bereta... Oh, a' he fato mo una spa'! El me avanza an dinari da balare.

A' vuò tornar a sentire se gi è andè via. [*Origlia di* 43 *nuovo all'uscio di Doralice*] A' no sento negun, gi è andè via fremamen. Oh, vegnesse sto vegio... [*In quella esce di nuovo Sier Tomao*]. Oh, laldò sia Dio, a' vegnerí pure! Stè a dar mente, che a' vuò andar a tuor le besenele... [*Si avvia alla porta*].

SIER TOMAO. Vate a far dar quele mie robe, e vien 44 presto. I miei zocoli fratoni, la mia bareta de note, i scofoni, l'albarelo da l'onguento per la mia siatica, e l'orinal; e varda no romper gniente.

RUZANTE. Poh, a' me le recorderè in lo culo tante 45 besenele!

SIER TOMAO. Ho asiao ogni cossa in portego. Vien 46 presto.

RUZANTE. Butè gi uoci in qua e in là, se 'l vegnesse mé 47 la so massarola, che la ne andesse çercanto. [*Va in casa*].

SIER TOMAO. Mo ben, va' via presto. [*Solo*] E' serò pur 48 contento, stasera; e' ho anche fato tanto che madona sè restà contenta. Ogni muodo, el sè stao bon aviso andar in vila, meio che qua, per mile boni respeti. E' 'nde son anche pí contento mi.

RUZANTE. [*torna in scena inciampando e imprecando, carico* 49 *delle robe di Sier Tomao*] Pota del caíre! Vegne el cancaro...

Let's see if I have enough money. [*He takes a fistful of coins from his pocket*]. Blast it, this is plenty! I don't want anyone to see me. This is a golden ducat from Venice, Venetian; this coin is Rhenish; silver pieces, copper pieces, pieces of six, and Austrian coppers. Damn, what a lot of money! Let me divide it: one pile is the hose, another pile the jacket, this one is the hat. What about the plume? Take a little from each pile . . . Oh, the sword? A little from the hose pile, a little from the jacket pile, a little from the cap . . . Oh, I've made a sword! And there's money left for dancing.

I'll go back to see if they've gone. [*He puts his ear to Doralice's door again*]. I don't hear anyone; they must have gone. Oh, if that old man would come . . . [*Sier Tomao comes out again*]. God be praised, you've come at last! Stay here and watch while I go get your things. [*He approaches the door*].

SIER TOMAO. Go have them give you my things and come right back. My wooden clogs, my nightcap, my slippers, the jar of unguent for my sciatica, and my urinal; and be careful not to break anything.

RUZANTE. Poh, I'll remember all that stuff on my backside!

SIER TOMAO. I put everything in the entrance. Return quickly.

RUZANTE. Look all around in case the maid comes looking for you. [*He enters the house*].

SIER TOMAO. Very well, go quickly. [*Alone*] I'll really be happy this evening; and I've done everything so that my lady will be content. In any case it was a good idea to go to the villa, better than here for a thousand good reasons. I feel better about it myself.

RUZANTE. [*returns on stage complaining and cursing, weighted down with Sier Tomao's belongings*] Twat of a fall! Pest consume him . . . The greater the hurry, the more the pest is in the way. Would you believe I broke the

Co' pí se ha priessia, el cancaro intanta pí. Te par mo,
che a' he roto e rinali e pitariti e 'l cancaro? Che cancaro
la magne, la no vêa l'ora de mandarme fuora de ca', st'altra: «Va' presto, tuòghe mo su...» A' no dego saer che la
l'ha fato vegnir in ca', el so berton? Vegna el cancaro...
squaso che a' no dissi, a' m'he sbregò un zenuogio. La
pianzea, co' a' partí, adesso la sgrigna, cancaro a ela e i
suò berton! [*A Sier Tomao, brusco*] Moa, avième inanzo,
presto, e caminè.

SIER TOMAO. Hastu ogni cossa?   50

RUZANTE. Missier sí, caminè pur via.

SIER TOMAO. Hastu i zocoli fratoni?   51

RUZANTE. Missier sí, a' he ogni cossa, caminè.

SIER TOMAO. Hastu la mia bareta de note?   52

RUZANTE. Missier sí, cancaro a le berete, caminè che   53
a' le zonzàn, caminè.

SIER TOMAO. Hastu i scofoni?   54

RUZANTE. Missier sí, che i dego pur aére... [Caminè],   55
pota del cancaro, che andagàn in la barca don' le va ele,
caminè, caminè.

SIER TOMAO. Hastu tuti do i scofoni?

RUZANTE. Missier sí, a' cherzo de sí, cancaro a i sco-   56
foni! Caminè, fé i passi lunghi.

SIER TOMAO. Hastu l'albarelo da l'onguento?   57

RUZANTE. A' 'l tussi pure, caminè, caminè.   58

SIER TOMAO. Ti no ha zà roto gniente, no?   59

RUZANTE. Roto gnente no, caminè, missier no,   60
caminè.

SIER TOMAO. La mia çinquedea l'hastu tolta?   61

RUZANTE. Tolte le maneze, ogni cossa, caminè...   62

SIER TOMAO. No digo i vanti, la storta...   63

RUZANTE. A' falón la via, cancaro a i stuorti e a i driti! 64
Andagón de qua, che l'è pí curta. [*Esce in quinta, seguito
da Sier Tomao*].

urinal, the bottles, the very pestilence? Pest consume her, she couldn't wait to get me out of the house, that woman: "Hurry up, pick it up . . ." And don't I know that she's had her fancy man come in the house? Pest consume . . . don't make me say it; I've skinned my knee. She was crying when I left; now she's grinning, pest take her and her fancy men! [*To Sier Tomao, brusquely*] Up, go ahead, quick, move.

SIER TOMAO. Do you have everything?

RUZANTE. Yes, master, move along.

SIER TOMAO. Do you have my wooden clogs?

RUZANTE. Yes, master, I have everything, move.

SIER TOMAO. Do you have my nightcap?

RUZANTE. Master yes, pox on caps, move so we can join them, move.

SIER TOMAO. Do you have my slippers?

RUZANTE. Yes, master, I must have them . . . Move, blasted twat, so we can get on the boat with them, move, move.

SIER TOMAO. Do you have both slippers?

RUZANTE. Yes master, I think so, blast the slippers! Move, take long steps.

SIER TOMAO. Do you have my flask of unguent?

RUZANTE. Certainly I took it, move, move.

SIER TOMAO. You didn't break anything, did you?

RUZANTE. Break anything, no, move, no master, move.

SIER TOMAO. My sheath, did you bring it?

RUZANTE. I took your finger warmers, everything, move.

SIER TOMAO. Not my glove, my sword, the curved one . . .

RUZANTE. We're going the wrong way, pox on curved swords and straight ones too! Let's go this way, it's shorter. [*He goes offstage, followed by Sier Tomao*].

161

Notes to the Text

Interlocutori

1. *Tancredi, Teodoro, Gismondo / Isotta, and Ginevra:* The reference their names and stories make to Boccaccio's *Decameron* and Pietro Bembo's *Gl'Asolani* is discussed in the Introduction.

2. *Doralice:* A model of the "cortigiana onesta," a courtesan appreciated for her conversational, musical, literary, or artistic skills.

3. *Ruzante:* His part was played by the author-actor Angelo Beolco, who took the name Ruzante on stage and in private life. The name Ruzante has existed among inhabitants of the countryside north of Padua since the sixteenth century. Ruzante's language, Pavano, is adapted from the dialect spoken by natives of the region and is the prevailing language spoken in the plays.

Prologo I

1. *la cortesia de un spirito valeroso:* May refer either to Ruzante's patron, Alvise Cornaro, or to the author, who perceived eternity in the timeless moment of performance.

2. *Il caso è nuovo:* The capture of a notorious Moorish corsair in 1533 would have been a current event if the play was written in 1533–1534.

Prologo II

1. The second prologue, in Pavano, is the kind of virtuoso monologue for which Ruzante was famous. The two prologues, one in Italian, the other in dialect, introduce the play's plurilingualism and its rhythm of high and low styles juxtaposed.

2. *Amore, per paura de' Turchi . . . è partú de Çipro:* War

between the Venetian empire and the Ottoman Turks began in the fifteenth century, and the threat of a Turkish invasion of Venice was felt throughout the first decades of the cinquecento. The Venetian victory at Lepanto in 1571 finally ended Turkish aggression in the eastern Mediterranean, although Cyprus was not saved. Cyprus is one of the largest islands in the Mediterranean over which Venice held sovereign power from 1489; in that year Caterina Cornaro, queen of Cyprus, abdicated in favor of the republic and, with her heir's safety guaranteed, retired to the town of Asolo, near Padua. Pietro Bembo made her court the setting of his dialogues on love called *Gl'Asolani* (1505). The notion that Love had left Cyprus because of the Turks may refer to the departure of Caterina Cornaro and her child, the former queen of Cyprus having been made a symbol of love by her courtier Bembo. The Homeric Aphrodite, goddess of fertility, is the mythological "Cyprian."

3. *cancaro:* One of Ruzante's frequently used expletives; it derives from the cinquecento formula of abuse meaning literally "canker consume you."

4. *roverso mondo (mondo rovescio):* "The world upside down" is a literary topic originating in antiquity.

5. *un servissio, con cossa che a' faesse mé:* Alludes to the topic of homosexuality or pederasty, repeated in act 3 with reference to university professors and students.

6. *Erunt duo in carne l'una:* The law is that of the Bible, which says: "Wherefore they are no more twain, but one flesh" (Matt. 19:6; also Gen. 2:24).

7. *comidiare vol dir magnare:* A play on the Latin verbs *comediare,* meaning "to write comedies," and *comedere,* meaning "to eat."

8. *quando muzàvimo per i Toíschi e per i Spagnaruoli:* In the first years of the wars of the League of Cambrai (1507–1509), farmers from the Pavano fled from

German and Spanish mercenaries in the army of the Emperor Maximilian I. The war continued after the Treaty of Noyen (1516), lasting until July 1518. Ruzante, as character, might have been captured when Maximilian attacked Padua in 1509. The author was presumably a young adolescent or child in 1509.

Act 1, Scene 1

1. *Le force de la pena sono . . . non hanno:* Taken verbatim from the *Decameron* VIII.vii: "Le forze della penna sono troppo maggiori che coloro non estimano che quelli con conoscimento provate non hanno."
2. *Madonna Laura, tanto lodata dal Petrarca:* The central theme of the 366 lyric poems in Petrarch's *Canzoniere* is the poet's love for Laura. Petrarch, born in Arezzo in 1304, spent the last years of his life (1370–1374) in Arquà, a town near Padua, where he is buried.

Act 2, Scene 2

1. *Aí pur el bel soran:* Ruzante had a "soprano" voice in the sense that he sang the top part in a four-part texture and carried the melody. In the cinquecento the treble or soprano clef was the common property of all high voices singing solo.
2. *ièrinu du, e sí a' cantàvino in quatro, e mi a' fasea de soran:* A melodic line for soprano or *cantus* (the top voice) could harmonize with a second melodic line for tenor, or a line for tenor could be paired with a line for countertenor; thus two lines, overlapping in range, provided both a harmonic foundation and a harmonizing part. Two other voices might be taken up by an accompanying musical instrument such as the lute to round out a four-part texture.
3. *assè dito che a' sonàvino sogoluoti o pivi de feraresi: So-*

goluoti (pifferi) are shawms, double-reed woodwind instruments used from the late thirteenth to the seventeenth century, forerunners of the modern oboe; *pive* are bagpipes. Shawms and bagpipes were often played together.

Act 2, Scene 4

1. *stramboti o barzelete:* The *strambotto,* a lyric of eight lines sung to tunes of sober rhythms (usually a new tune each time the piece was sung), was highly regarded in the fifteenth century, especially in its courtly formulations; see N. Pirrotta, *Music and Culture in Italy from the Middle Ages to the Baroque* (Cambridge: Harvard University Press, 1984), pp. 75–76, 146–148. The *barzelletta* is a popular form of lyric poetry with any number of lines, usually of eight syllables, having a popular flavor; see Pirrotta, *Music and Culture in Italy,* pp. 77, 146.
2. *Stramuoti:* Plays on the serious tone of the *strambotto.*
3. *Sgnanferlati:* A name invented from *sgananfo,* an onomatopoetic term for someone who speaks through his nose.
4. "La mala morte": This canzone is the one Ruzante sings with Menato in act 5, scene 1; it is mentioned also in *La Betìa* and may have been a favorite or signature song. Ruzante's third song, "Levami de una bela matina," is published in Emilio Lovarini, "Le canzoni popolari in Ruzzante e in altri scrittori alla pavana del secolo XVI," *Studi sul Ruzzante e sulla letteratura pavana,* ed. Gianfranco Folena (Padua: Antenore, 1965), pp. 181–182. The words are from a refrain for which music has been found and published by Nino Pirrotta in *Li due Orfei* (Turin: Eri, 1969), pp. 115–116.
5. "El papa sí ha concesso quindese ani": A *strambotto* by Leonardo Giustinian (1388–1446), a Venetian composer or troubadour poet who wrote a number of eight-line lyrics and gave his name to the genre

called *giustiniane*. The text is published in M. Dazzi, *Leonardo Giustinian, poeta popolare d'amore* (Bari: Laterza, 1934), p. 104.

6. "Andemo, amanti, tuti in Barbaria" : A *strambotto* by Panfilo Sassi of Modena (1454?–1527).

7. "Quatro sospiri te voria mandare" : A *strambotto* by Leonardo Giustinian.

8. *Rigobelo (Arrigobello):* A clown, especially one who urged people to come to the show.

Act 3, Scene 1

1. *Studio:* The University of Padua was called the Studio in the sixteenth century. Active from 1222, the university closed during the war of Cambrai and reopened in 1517.

Act 3, Scene 2

1. *per segrè:* Before the Napoleonic decree of Saint-Cloud in 1806 churchyards were used for burial grounds; thus "graveyards" is intended. See Ruzante, *Teatro,* ed. L. Zorzi (Turin: Einaudi, 1967), p. 1471.

2. *Sòstene:* This name has been interpreted as Demosthenes and Socrates as well as Aristotle.

3. *Amore no è altro che potinzia e desidierio:* Bembo defines love as desire ("*desio*") in *Gl'Asolani* III. v, a notion he rejected in the 1530 edition of *Gl'Asolani* (III. xiii). In the myth of Legraçion, Ruzante refers to Plato's *Symposium* where Socrates tells how Eros was born to Ποροσ (Resource) and Πηνια (Poverty, Need, Desire).

Act 4, Scene 1

1. *Capua:* A town in Campania, in the province of Caserta, where Frederick II erected a castle. The sta-

tues that decorated the castle were contemporary imitations of classical sculptures.

2. *catar l'anconeta . . . De Anconeta:* The word play is on Ancona, a city on the Adriatic coast, and *anconeta,* indicating an altar painting.

3. *an a la divisa, le calçe:* Decorative hose with an embroidered device or band of color worn by members of youthful confraternities like the Companies of the Hose. Young men attired in hose of this type appear in Carpaccio's painting of the life of Saint Ursula.

Act 4, Scene 2

1. *Gagieta (Gaeta):* A seaport town in Campania, in the province of Caserta.

2. *Messer Gabrioto de gli Onesti . . . mona Dionora di Neri:* Names that appear in the *Decameron. Gabrioto* appears in IV. vi; *gli Onesti,* in V. viii; and *Dionora,* in X. v.

Act 4, Scene 3

1. *Marco, Marco:* The war cry of the army of the Republic of Venice. Saint Mark is the patron saint of Venice.

2. *el triàbiti:* Corruption of the Latin *qui habitat,* indicating Psalm 40.

3. *mi andasea da i pivi:* At out-of-door festivities two or three musicians playing on bagpipes or other wind instruments accompanied the dance.

4. *pavana:* A dance indigenous to the Pavano, the pavan was (or became) sedate in character. Ruzante's choreography, with his right foot extended, is unusual as the choreography generally began with the left foot forward. The dance songs that accompanied the pavan were sung or played in four-part harmony.

5. *polenta, peverà e faveta: Polenta* is a food made of

cornmeal cooked in boiling salted water, stirred constantly until it reaches such a consistency that it can be cut into slices. In the countryside and mountain areas of northern Italy, polenta substitutes for bread. Hot polenta may be eaten with vegetables such as *peverà* (peppers) and *faveta* (broad green beans).

6. *bon ano:* Literally, "good year"; a formula for saying good-bye.

7. *tandem:* Latin adverb indicating *pray? then?* in interrogations.

8. *Santa Cataruza:* Diminutive for Saint Catherine. According to legend, Saint Catherine was a well-born, well-schooled maiden of Alexandria, who protested against the worship of idols. Having defeated the arguments of fifty philosophers, she was martyred when she refused to deny her faith and marry the emperor, called Maxentius. In Padua, the church of Saint Catherine was begun in the early thirteenth century. Saint Catherine was patron of the university's law students, who organized the procession on her feast day, November 25.

9. *Rolando:* The Roland or Orlando celebrated in Boiardo's *Orlando innamorato* and in Ariosto's *Orlando furioso*.

Act 4, Scene 5

1. *Cope, Fiorin: Coppe* is one of the four suits in an Italian deck of cards; the florin is a golden coin first produced in Florence in 1252; it became the basic unit of the Florentine monetary system.

2. *Arquà:* A town in the Euganean hills where Petrarch lived from 1370 until his death in 1374. His burial place is there.

3. *Lire de grossi, o de pízoli:* The *grossi* were large silver coins minted extensively by Enrico Dandolo at a weight of 2.18 grams and .965 pure silver. From about 1350 to 1520 the old *grosso* was replaced by

169

silver coins of changing weight and purity, often named for the doge issuing them.

4. *smozanighi (mocenighi)* and *marçie[gi] (marcelli):* Throughout this period silver maintained a stable value relative to gold (eleven to one) and was the money of account in Venetian government obligations and trade. Purchases, wages, and debts were calculated in *lire di pizoli* (*piccoli*), smaller coins containing less silver. For payment of large sums the larger silver *grosso* or gold ducats were obviously more convenient than coins of lesser value.

Act 5, Scene 3

1. *Tamen:* Latin particle indicating *still, yet.*

Act 5, Scene 4

1. *ducato d'oro . . . scarantani:* The golden ducat, later called *zecchino,* was minted in Venice without interruption from 1284 under Doge Giovanni Dandolo until 1797 under Doge Ludovico Vanin, the last doge of the Venetian Republic. The *rainese* is a Rhenish florin; *cavaluoti* (*cavallotti*) are silver pieces showing a saint or a person *a cavallo* (on horseback). *Moragie* (*moraglie*) are copper pieces from Emilia or the Marches; *da sie beçe* (*pezzi da sei soldi*) are pieces of six; *[s]carantani* are copper coins of little value, mined in Austria in the sixteenth century. In the days of the wars of the League of Cambrai, silver and gold coins were scarce and foreign coins appeared frequently in Venice.

Bibliography

BÀRATTO, MARIO. "Da Ruzante al Beolco: Per la storia di un autore." *Atti del convegno sul tema: La poesia rusticana nel Rinascimento.* Problemi attuali di scienza e di cultura. Rome: Accademia Nazionale dei Lincei, 1969.

————. "Ruzante." In *Tre saggi sul teatro.* Venice: Neri Pozza, 1964. Originally published as "L'esordio di Ruzante," *Revue des études italiennes,* n.s., 3 (1956): 92–162.

BROWN, HOWARD M. "The Genesis of a Style: The Parisian Chanson, 1500–1530." In *Chanson and Madrigal, 1480–1530,* ed. James Haar. Cambridge: Harvard University Press, 1964.

CALENDOLI, GIOVANNI. "Antefatti di una fortuna difficile." In *Ruzante sulle scene italiane del secondo dopoguerra.* Catalog for the exhibition at the Oratorio di San Rocco in Padua, May 25–June 15, 1983, sponsored by the Comune di Padova, Assessorato allo Spettacolo, and the Università degli Studi di Padova, Istituto di Storia del Teatro e dello Spettacolo.

————. *Ruzante.* Venice: Corbo e Fiore, 1985.

CALENDOLI, GIOVANNI, AND GIUSEPPE VELLUCCI, eds. *Convegno internazionale di studi sul Ruzante.* Venice: Corbo e Fiore, 1987.

CLUBB, LOUISE GEORGE. "Woman as Wonder." In *Studies in the Continental Background of Renaissance English Literature,* ed. Dale B. J. Randall and George Walton Williams. Durham, N.C.: Duke University Press, 1977.

DEBOSIO, GIANFRANCO. "Un trentennio di lavoro sul Ruzante." In *Convegno internazionale di studi sul Ruzante,* ed. Giovanni Calendoli and Giuseppe Vellucci. Venice: Corbo e Fiore, 1987. Originally published in *Ruzante sulle scene italiane del secondo dopoguerra.* Catalog for the exhibition at the Oratorio di San Rocco in Padua, May 25–June 15, 1983, sponsored by the Comune di Padova, Assessorato allo Spettacolo, and the Università degli Studi di Padova, Istituto di Storia del Teatro e dello Spettacolo.

171

DELLA TERZA, DANTE. Introduction to *Arcadia and the Stage: An Introduction to the Dramatic Art of Angelo Beolco, Called Ruzante,* by Nancy Dersofi. Madrid: Porrua; Washington, D.C., Studia Humanitatis, 1978.

DERSOFI, NANCY. "Angelo Beolco." In *The New Grove Dictionary of Music and Musicians,* ed., Stanley Sadie. London: Macmillan, 1980.

———. "Le canzoni del Ruzante e l'*Anconitana.*" In *Convegno internazionale di studi sul Ruzante,* ed. Giovanni Calendoli and Giuseppe Velluci. Venice: Corbo e Fiore, 1987.

———. "Comic Reflections." In *Renaissance Studies in Honor of Craig Hugh Smyth,* ed. Andrew Morrogh. Florence: Giunti Barbera, 1985.

LOGAN, OLIVER. *Culture and Society in Venice, 1470–1790.* New York: Scribner's, 1972.

LOVARINI, EMILIO. *Studi sul Ruzzante e sulla letteratura pavana,* ed. Gianfranco Folena. Padua: Antenore, 1965.

MENEGAZZO, E. "Tre scritti di Alvise Cornaro." In *Tra Latino e Volgare* per Carlo Dionisotti. *Medioevo e Umanesimo* 17–18 (1974): 585–613.

MENEGAZZO, E., AND P. SAMBIN. "Nuove esplorazioni archivistiche per Angelo Beolco e Alvise Cornaro." *Italia medioevale e umanistica* 7 (1964): 133–247, and 9 (1966): 229–385.

MESSIBUGO, CHRISTOFARO DI. *Banchetti, composizioni di vivande e apparecchio generale.* Ferrara, 1549. Facsimile, ed. F. Bandini, Venice: Pozza, 1960.

MILANI, MARISA. "Rileggendo Ruzzante: Note, ipotesi e provocazioni." In *Filologia veneta.* Vol. 1, *Ruzzante.* Padova: Editoriale Programma, 1988.

———. "Snaturalitè e deformazione nella lingua teatrale del Ruzante." In *Lingue e strutture del teatro italiano del Rinascimento.* Padua: Liviana, 1970.

MORTIER, ALFRED. *Ruzzante.* Vol. 1. Paris: J. Peyronnet, 1925.

PADOAN, GIORGIO. "L'*Anconitana* tra Boccaccio, Bibbiena e Ariosto." In *Momenti del Rinascimento veneto.* Padua: Antenore, 1978. Originally published in *Lettere italiane* 22 (1970): 100–105.

———. "Angelo Beolco da Ruzante a Perduoçimo." In *Mo-*

menti del Rinascimento veneto. Padua: Antenore, 1978. Originally published in *Lettere italiane* 20 (1968): 121–200.

PIRROTTA, NINO. *Music and Culture in Italy from the Middle Ages to the Baroque.* Cambridge: Harvard University Press, 1984.

PIRROTTA, NINO, AND ELENA POVOLEDO. *Music and Theatre from Poliziano to Monteverdi.* New York: Cambridge University Press, 1975. Translation of *Li due Orfei* (Turin: Eri, 1969; new edition, Turin: Einaudi, 1975).

RUZANTE. *Teatro.* Ed. Ludovico Zorzi. Turin: Einaudi, 1967.

SLIM, H. COLIN. "Two Paintings of 'Concert Scenes' from the Veneto and the Morgan Library's Unique Music Print of 1520." In *In Cantu et in Sermone: For Nino Pirrotta on His 80th Birthday,* ed. F. Della Seta and F. Piperno. Florence: Olschki, 1989.

ZORZI, LUDOVICO. "Canzoni inedite del Ruzante." *Atti del Istituto Veneto di Scienze, Lettere ed Arti* 119 (1960–1961): 25–73.

———. "Tra Ruzzante e Vitruvio." In *Alvise Cornaro e il suo tempo.* Padua: Antoniana, 1980.

Biblioteca Italiana
The First Bilingual Editions

GIAMBATTISTA DELLA PORTA
Gli Duoi Fratelli Rivali
The Two Rival Brothers
Edited and translated
by Louise George Clubb
1980
*

TOMMASO CAMPANELLA
La Città del Sole:
Dialogo Poetico
The City of the Sun:
A Poetical Dialogue
Translated by Daniel J. Donno
1981
*

TORQUATO TASSO
Tasso's Dialogues:
A Selection
with the Discourse on
the Art of the Dialogue
Translated by Carnes Lord
and Dain A. Trafton
1982
*

GIACOMO LEOPARDI
Operette Morali
Essays and Dialogues
Translated by Giovanni Cecchetti
1983
*

CARLO COLLODI
Le Avventure di Pinocchio
The Adventures of Pinocchio
Translated with an Introduction
and Notes by Nicolas J. Perella
1986
*

MATTEO MARIA BOIARDO
Orlando Innamorato
Translated with an Introduction and Notes
by Charles Stanley Ross
1989

Compositor:	G & S Typesetters
Text:	10/12 Bembo
Display:	Bembo
Printer and Binder:	Thomson-Shore